I0119123

Reflections from

KOSOVO

Reflections from
KOSOVO

Edited by

FATON TONY BISLIMI

ERIC FRANCO, Ed.D.

Contributors:

Danielle Gregoire

Roderick Kelly

Evan Klein

Anneka Sutton

Ally Whittaker

The Balkans
FREE PRESS
International Publishing House

Edmonton | Houston

THE BALKANS FREE PRESS
www.balkansfreepress.com

Copyright © 2014 by authors, editors, and contributors.

All rights reserved.

ISBN-13: 978-0988160835
ISBN-10: 0988160838
Printed in Canada and the United States of America

This book is based on contributions by participants of the
Balkans Peace Program – Summer 2013. This program was
implemented and administered by the Bislimi Group Foundation
and took place in May and early June 2013 in Gjilan, Kosovo.

Proceeds from this book go to support the Balkans Peace
Program of the Bislimi Group Foundation.

For more information on the program or the foundation, please
visit: www.bislimi.org

Reflections from

KOSOVO

TABLE OF CONTENTS

ACKNOWLEDGEMENTS

I WOULD LIKE TO THANK all of the participants of the Balkans Peace Program – Summer 2013, some of whom travelled from half the way around the world to be part of this program: Griffin Cornwall, Danielle Gregoire, Roderick Kelly, Evan Klein, Kathryn Larin, Anneka Sutton, Amy Whittaker, and Milan Zavada. I would like to also thank the Kosovar host brothers and sisters and their families who made sure the foreign students on the program felt at home: Gazmend Azizi, Emira Biçkaj, Vigan Musliu, Flakron Rexhepaj, Festa Shabani, Erëblina Xhemaili, and Arben Zeqiri.

Special thanks go to Halit Bislimi and to all of my foundation's volunteers for their help in making this program a true success. Thanks go also to Milot Shkodra and the Gjilani University College for all their support.

My most heartfelt gratitude and appreciation are extended to the Speaker of the Parliament of Kosovo, Mr. Jakup Krasniqi; Deputy Prime Minister of Kosovo and former President of Kosovo, Mr. Behgjet Pacolli; Deputy Ministers Mr. Hajdin Abazi, and Mr. Nehat Mustafa; Mayor of Gjilan, Mr. Qemajl Mustafa, and other political and government officials who met with our BPP participants.

Special thanks go to Dr. Eric Franco of Waldorf College for being a co-editor and a special contributor to this book.

Lastly, I would have never been able to put this program as well as this book together without the endless love and support from my beautiful wife, Nora, and my princess daughters, Fiona and Olsa, as well as my parents and sisters.

Faton Tony Bislimi
Co-editor & Program Director for
the Balkans Peace Program

INTRODUCTION

WHEN I first thought about establishing a summer program for foreign students in Kosovo, I had several key ideas in mind. I wanted the program to be academic. I also wanted the program to be fun. The program also had to be culturally immersing. It had to include a tour of the neighbouring countries.

As I tried to put all of these requirements together into one program, I realized that while it may seem impossible, it can actually be done. So, I made sure the Balkans Peace Program would consist of three key components—academic, cultural, and educational.

To satisfy the first requirement—academic—students on the program would be offered an intensive (seminar-like) course on the theme of the program, namely international development, peacekeeping, peace-building, post-conflict reconstruction, state-building, etc.

To satisfy the second component—cultural immersion—I decided that the foreign students participating in the program would stay with local host families who would have a son or daughter of similar age and who speaks English to become the official host brother or host sister of the foreign student. Moreover, to diversify the class, I opened up the program (its academic component, the course) to local students with an interest in the topic and with good English proficiency.

To satisfy the third component—educational—the program would provide the students with a tour of not only Kosovo's key historic and natural attractions but also of some of the most renowned places of historic or touristic value in Kosovo's neighbouring countries of Montenegro, Albania, and Macedonia.

The Balkans Peace Program 2012 marked the beginning of this flagship program of my foundation, the Bislimi Group Foundation.

As this book is being completed, the third cohort (class of 2014) of the Balkans Peace Program is making their final preparations to head to Kosovo. Why Kosovo? Well, there are several characteristics that make Kosovo a unique place. Putting aside the very obvious reasons—such as the fact that Kosovo is my home country and I share an indescribable connection with it—Kosovo is unique both in terms of its history and the present developments. Despite being a rather small country in Europe, Kosovo is of international relevance, especially politically. During the Kosovo War of 1998-99, the world was bitterly divided on the issue of whether a military intervention by NATO was legal and just, as NATO embarked on a 78-day bombing campaign against Serbia in an effort to stop ethnic cleansing and mass murders against innocent ethnic Albanians in Kosovo.

Once the war ended, Kosovo was put under international administration headed by the UN. The UN Mission in Kosovo (UNMIK) became the legislative, administrative, and executive body governing Kosovo on the basis of the UN Security Council Resolution 1244 of June 1999. This was the first time in the history of the UN that the UN had undertaken such an ambitious role—to actually govern a territory.

From an international relations perspective, NATO's intervention to save Kosovo and UN's taking over to govern it, for instance, show the uniqueness of Kosovo.

Moreover, Kosovo is unique also in the way it has undertaken its state-building process. Kosovo is the only country in Europe in which over half of the population is under the age of twenty-five. Kosovo is, unfortunately, the poorest country in Europe as well.

On February 17, 2008, Kosovo declared its independence and thus far it has been recognized by over 100 nations around the world. Yet, Kosovo is not a member of the UN and, as a result, cannot participate in many international sports events as a nation.

Over 90% of Kosovo's population is made up by ethnic Albanians, with about 8% being ethnic Serbs and the rest being of Roma, Ashkali, Egyptian, Turkish and other ethnic origins.

Yet, Kosovo is defined as a multi-ethnic state and provides its minority communities with some of the most advanced rights, constitutionally guaranteed.

Kosovo is a great place to be if you are interested in studying post-conflict societies, international development or related topics. It is located in Europe; it is safe; and it is developing.

So, it provides the right environment for students with an interest in topics such as those aforementioned. And, I am certain that the Balkans Peace Program participants enjoyed their Kosovo experience.

In this book, apart from the first chapter by Dr. Franco, which is a way of giving the reader a better understanding of the importance of education, *the right education*, especially for a country such as Kosovo, the history of which has been interpreted, used, and abused in so many ways; the rest of the chapters are original contributions by the BPP 2013 participants.

I am very thankful to Danielle Gregoire (a fourth year political science major at the University of Alberta), Roderick Kelly (an MA candidate in War Studies at the Royal Military College of Canada), Evan Klein (a philosophy and religion major, also completing a certificate in Peace and Post-Conflict Resolution at the University of Alberta), Anneka Sutton (a second year political science and global studies major at the Sir Wilfrid Laurier University), and Ally Whittaker (a fourth year history and English major at the University of Alberta) for sharing their Kosovo experience with us. As you will see, they all came out of the program with a different take. They all have different perspectives on many things and issues. While their stories are personal, together they tell the story of Kosovo. As diverse as these stories' perspectives are, so is the actual life in Kosovo. Problems and issues coexist with hope, optimism, and good things.

Faton Tony Bislimi

18 May 2014

The Transformative Effect of History Education: Using History Education to Promote Regional Stability and Identity in the Balkans

Dr. Eric Franco

Abstract

History education in the Balkans is a politically charged issue which often results in hostility toward groups or individuals of whom may question one's national history as fact. This is especially true for Kosovo, Europe's newest and most fragile democracy where its physical location rests at the intersection of a complex nexus of multiethnic, linguistic, religious, and political tension yet to be resolved. For Kosovo, the implementation of a quality history program based not on nationalistic grand narratives, but one which rests on a foundation of inquiry is needed. The use of the region's rich primary sources and teachers qualified in developing quality history curricula which maintains the discipline's integrity while, at the same time, creating learning environments which facilitate high levels of student engagement presents significant substantive potential for the development of Kosovo's national identity. On a much broader scale, such a history education program in the Balkans would be "bleeding edge," as its current history educational pro forma is but a remnant of the nationalistic Yugoslavian system centered on high levels of pan-Albanianism. Developing a national history program predicated on critical thinking, multiple source material, promoting social voice and multiple perspectives has the potential for Kosovo leading the Balkans at developing a pan-Balkan identity sans political grand narratives. Moreover, the development and establishment of such practice may lead to educators and scholars alike to rethink the term, "Balkanization." Rather than its present connotation of extreme divisiveness, "Balkanization" could be transformed into a renewed meaning of reconciliation and 21st century regional identity.

One Region, Many Peoples, Many Worlds – Whose Kosovo Is It?

The issue of identity and stability in the Balkans has been of grave concern throughout the 19th and 20th centuries among the disparate peoples and political entities in the region. As strong 19th century Balkan nationalist movements rallied for their own interests, and as the Austro-Hungarian forces rivalled the Ottoman Empire for the region, other nations (France and Russia, for example) took advantage of the socio-political instability for their own self-interests. We see this occur in the encouragement of pan-Slavism in the Balkans as Russia claimed historical and ethnic ties to Serbians; we see this as Ottomans pushed their influence among the predominantly Gheg Albanian Muslims to counter Slavic nationalism. We see the French support the Austro-Hungarians as a mere geopolitical thumbscrew against Russia. We see this in the "settling" of Balkan disputes at the 1878 Treaty of Berlin, among others. Clearly, third-party powers in the 19th and early 20th centuries fanned the flames of ethnic and religious sectarianism – a socio-political phenomenon that didn't truly exist in the modern sense prior to the onset of the 19th century. On the contrary, much of the pre-19th century experiences of Gheg Albanians, Serbs, Vlachs, Macedonians, Greeks, Montenegrins, and Bosnians – Christians and Muslims, and others, shared a relatively peaceful coexistence in the region and arguably, a convergence of shared lifestyle and experience that may be construed as a pre-nationalist pan-Balkan culture.[1] Of this, peasant goat, sheep, and pig farming were common means to make a meagre living off of the land, as extended families often worked together for the collective good. This was largely true for many ethnic groups in the Balkans, as agrarianism, both before and during Ottoman rule, remained largely unchanged as traditional means of subsistence as a feudal system even in the industrial era.[2] This is somewhat similar today throughout Kosovo and parts of southern Serbia, as small towns and villages continue to farm crops and domesticated animals, albeit on a small scale. But how did the region succumb to the forces of hyper-charged nationalism, which seems to characterize the Balkans as the perfect example of social, political, ethnic, religious, and linguistic fracturing and hostility toward one another? Moreover, how does one even begin to wrap one's head around the deep-rooted enmity to the point to which the term, *Balkanization,* is often used as a succinct transitive verb to describe the continued separation and hostility among a people. Therefore, illuminating various elements of a traditional pan-Balkan shared identity alongside traditional points of division is relatively easy, given the well-documented history of the region over the past four-hundred

---

[1] Glenny, *The Balkans: Nationalism, War, and the Great Powers, 1804-1999.*
[2] ibid

years. But how can modern changes in history education (both for teacher preparation and for public school students) help promote the establishment and development of a renewed pan-Balkan identity relying on current best disciplinary practices. It is through this lens that the traditional and outdated nationalistic grand narratives will give way to an educational approach, which will lead to regional stability.

While there were clear ethnic and religious delineations among the various ethnic and religious groups, social and economic intercourse was a normative and mutually beneficial experience for most. The influence of the third-party powers such as the Ottoman Empire, while injecting Turkish culture, architecture, governance, and religion into the region from the 14th-early 20th centuries, was an experience shared by all indigenous Balkan peoples. Misha Glenny claims, the Ottoman rule in the northern edge of Serbia made many enemies as the Ottomans' unrestrained brutality on the part of the Janissaries left an intense hatred for the Turks.[3] Arguably, Serbian society was relatively stable and self-contained until the Turkish Janissaries disrupted their lives. The resulting anti-Muslim sentiments compelled Serbs to take to the countryside to fight an insurgent war against the Turks. Bosnians, Albanians, and others at times shared this sentiment and at times fought alongside one

---

[3] Malcolm, *Kosovo: A Short History.*

another against the Turks. Such a common enemy might draw disparate peoples closer together, but Ottoman repression was often very heavy-handed, especially at the Serbs, who saw Ottoman reprisals as an all-out war against Serbian Orthodox Christians. As in the so-called, "Slaughter of the Kneezes," where several Serbian chieftains were killed in an effort to nullify Serbian resistance, the Turks' actions had the reverse effect. But the Ottoman slaughter served as a turning point, as the Serbian rebellion that followed marked the beginning of *modern nationalism* in the Balkans. However, as historian, Noel Malcolm reminds us, "the popular view of Ottoman rule is almost entirely negative" and he goes on to reject this popular claim, as this perspective fails to acknowledge the political, administrative, and infrastructural *improvements* within the region by the Ottomans' desire to establish permanent territorial claim. Be that as it may, the popular history of Ottoman oppression and delineated identity of non-Turks remains imbued deep in the psyche of people in the Balkans. Exacerbated by political and nationalistic forces in the region, one common sentiment in the Balkans dismisses Turkish relative toleration as invaders, aggressors, occupiers, and conquerors. But the positive enduring legacy of Ottoman tolerance is easily seen in the southwest Kosovar city of Prizren, where Gheg Albanian and Turkish influences have, over the centuries, converged to create a rich polyethnic atmosphere where one needn't be Turk, Albanian, Serb, Muslim, or Christian to enjoy the diffusion of its cultures. Indeed, Turko-Albanian cultural diffusion is easily seen in various foods, clothing, architecture, mosques, and family names. But over the past two centuries, the upsurge in political nationalism, as it spread throughout Central Europe, eventually made its way into the Balkans as the Austro-Hungarians sought to expel the Turks and expand the Hapsburg dynasty in the Balkans Peninsula.

A casual observer might assume the expansion of the Austro-Hungarians into the Balkans would be a more welcome sight, as they pushed the Ottomans out of Bosnia and other areas in the region. But Serbian resistance against the Austro-Hungarians was just as fierce as it was toward the Turks, and a strong sense of Serbian nationalism, as in so many other stories of heroic national causes, resulted in an overinflated sense of their social and political privilege. But Serbs were not the only peoples to resist the subjugation of foreign peoples in their lands and not all indigenous peoples resisted the Turks or Austro-Hungarians. Such is the case among many Kosovo Albanians whose adoption of Islam granted a marginally elevated status among other peoples in the region.[4] But even in this case, the motivation for religious conversion was for monetary gain or land acquisition. Similarly, Bosnian Muslims shared similar privilege, although in the eyes of the Turks, they were still

---

[4] Zefi, *Islamiazation of Albanians Through Centuries*.

subjugates.[5] The resulting cultural imprint is, therefore, a multicultural region with a checkered past where foreign occupation impacted the insurgents just as much as the confederates, although in different ways and, as we will see, for different ends.

Despite such a rich and multicultural history, the 1878 League of Prizren underscores the different means to different ends. By the mid-19th century, the deep-rooted sense of singular identity among the peoples in the region and Prizren in particular present a harbinger for the Balkans' story of the 20th century. But ethnic identity and its socio-historical claim to the Balkans is not a story exclusive to the Ottomans or Albanians as the Serbs' popular memory of their historical connection to Kosovo as their self-initiated exile from the region and the mid-southern Balkans to escape Islamic subjugation, promoted their own renewed sense of ethnic and religious nationalism. [6] Sentiments and actions such as these pushed the political buttons which led to the 1912-1913 Balkans War, a conflict where a pan-Balkan coalition, known as the Balkan League, consisting of Serbia, Bulgaria, Greece, and Montenegro set to oust Ottoman rule in the Balkans. Unfortunately, the delineated Balkan identities and self-interests of the coalition partners led to fighting among

---

[5] Ibid.

[6] Miller and Kagan, "The Great Powers and Regional Conflicts: Eastern Europe and the Balkans from Post-Nepoleonic Era to the Post-Cold War Era."

themselves, resulting in the Second Balkans War (June-August of 1913). In its aftermath, Serbia's position in the Balkans was elevated to the most prominent position with its military power, which subsequently called to expel the Austro-Hungarians from Bosnia-Herzegovina. Of course, the tensions between the two led to the spark that ignited the Great War in June, 1914 and in its aftermath at the Paris Peace Conference that such complex and deep-rooted ideations of ethnic identity that led to the establishment the failed 1918 "Versailles state" of the Kingdom of Serbs, Croats, and Slovenes and the rise of the consolidated Yugoslavia in 1929 under King Alexander I. Under Alexander, oppression and alienation of non-Serbian peoples continued up to the German invasion of Yugoslavia in 1941.

Such patterns of nationalistic tension endured throughout the 20th century, as Serbia became the epicenter of Balkans governance under the second consolidated political sovereign of Yugoslavia under Josip Broz Tito. This new Yugoslavia sought to promote a new "brotherhood and peace" and reignited the region's Serbian ethnic heritage while, at the same time, marginalized other ethnic peoples such as Kosovo Albanians and others. For example, while Tito's promotion of Yugoslavian development resulted in urban infrastructure, functional social and political institutions, manufacturing facilities, and a robust university system, he largely neglected to develop Albanian or other Muslim-dominated areas, such as

Kosovo.[7] Moreover, as one must note, even under Tito's Yugoslavia, Kosovo remained the poorest and most underdeveloped province in the country. But it was through the propaganda of a unified Yugoslavia and, to greater extent, the repressive measures ushered to mitigate ethnic uprisings within the country.[8] It would be such tension that would resurface following Tito's death in 1980, as the eventual political forces under Slobodan Milosevic's leadership, fanned the flames of Serbian ethnic nationalism throughout the 1980s to create a *Greater Serbia* and, at the expulsion of non-Serbs in Serb-populated areas. Moreover, as we seen in the ultra-nationalistic and politically charged rhetoric of Milosevic's Gazimestan Speech delivered on the 600th anniversary of the battle of Kosovo Polje, the most significant event in Serbia's historical claim to Kosovo.[9] In his effort to exalt Serbian unification, and regional unity at-large, Milosevic remarked,

"What has been certain through all the centuries until our time today is that disharmony struck Kosovo 600 years ago. If we lost the battle, then this was not only the result of social superiority and the armed advantage of the Ottoman Empire but also of the tragic disunity in the leadership of the Serbian state at that time." [10]

---

[7] Glenny, *The Balkans: Nationalism, War, and the Great Powers, 1804-1999.*

[8] Judah, *Kosovo: What Everyone Needs to Know.*

[9] Judah, *The Serbs: History, Myth and the Destruction of Yugoslavia.*

[10] Milosevic, "SLOBODAN MILOSEVIC'S 1989 ST. VITUS DAY SPEECH."

His nationalistic words, tailored for the Serbian minority in the region, catalyst for regional rejection of Serbia's attempt to tighten its control over the disparate peoples the region. Beginning and ending Kosovo, his words of unification under a post-Tito Serbian government sowed the seeds of the dissolution of Yugoslavia and a series of wars in Balkans throughout the 1990s.

But the significance of these events, compounded by the multicultural development of the region must not be a zero-sum narrative by victors or losers of the tumultuous political power-plays and subjugation of the Balkan peoples by various forces of nationalism and ethnocentrism. On the contrary, the rich and multifaceted story of the Balkans provides an ideal backdrop for deep historical study of the region's social development, the development of rule of law, the impact the hyperpower expansion of the Ottomans had in the region and its subsequent cultural diffusion, the consequences of polarized nationalism, war, ethnic tension and much more! As the Balkan peoples endured the political changes throughout the 20th century, more wars, communist subjugation, hypernationalism, and the dissolution of Yugoslavia with nearly a decade of war, underscore the reality of various perspectives of the multicultural peninsula have had a long, hard, and tragic story coupled with a vibrantly rich diverse and resilient people. How, then, can history education foster a renewed sense of identity and regional stability?

The Politics of Education

History education in the Balkans is a politically charged issue that often results in hostility toward groups or individuals of whom may question one's perspective or, "telling," of the region's national memory. This is especially true for Kosovo, Europe's newest and most fragile democracy where, despite its current Albanian majority, its physical location rests at the intersection of a complex nexus of multiethnic, linguistic, religious, and political tension having yet to be resolved. As seen in the recent example of modern Turkey's political nudging to rewrite the grand narrative of the Ottoman entry in the Balkans, major revisions of Kosovo's history textbooks reflect the extra-national interest in regional identity through the vehicle of history education.[11] I must point out that such revisions were made without the cognizance or consultation of the history textbook authors. According to Kosovo Ministry of Education history curriculum consultants as well as a recent Balkan Insight (Balkan Investigative Reporting Network) report, Turkey's response to the traditional Tito or Hoxha narratives was anything but supportive. In 2010, Turkey pulled all of their funding for

---

[11] Musliu, "Kosovo Textbooks Soften Line on Ottoman Rule :: Balkan Insight."

Kosovar history textbooks due to language considered undermining to Turkey's national heritage and damaging her influence in the region until further agreement on the grand narrative could be reached. In short, Turkey, or should I say, Turkish money prevailed. Turkey's insistence on revising Kosovo's national and regional historical narrative to reflect almost 500 years of influence should, according to Turkish politicians such as Prime Minister Recep Tayyip Erdogan, illuminate the political motivation underlying Turkey's use of history education to reshape Kosovars' social and political identity. The effort is clear – dismantle the traditional Albanian mythology of Skanderbeg, Shota, Prishtina, or Serbian insurgents and their perception of Ottoman rule as oppressive and illegitimate. Historical interpretations, regardless of the historical record and regardless of the truth, must conform to how the Turks prefer to have others in the region view the Ottomans. To provide some concrete examples of such revisions, may I draw your attention to the excerpts lifted from the texts currently used for instruction in grades, 5, 6, and 8:

• Replacing "violence" and "killing" with "conquering" and "imprisonment," on page 62 of a fifth-grade textbook.

• Deleting the sentence: "Ottomans killed many Albanians," on page 69 of the same book.

• Replacing "Ruthless Ottoman rule" with the more neutral sounding "Ottoman conquest" on page 83 of the sixth-grade history textbook.

• Replacing "They applied strict measures against non-Muslim people" with "All citizens in the countries conquered by the Ottoman Empire, in the daily lives, were equal before the law."

As one can clearly see, word-choice underscores the likely motivation for such revisions. In many ways, such language reflects the politicization of history education in a manner not too different from that of American textbook narratives. However, at its academic core, history education is *not* about grand narratives to serve some greater political purpose. If we can agree that history is *not* the promotion of a single narrative, but rather, *history is a study of the past*, then such calls to question the purpose of history education in the first place. Is it to indoctrinate or is it to educate? If indoctrinate, then we needn't discuss the issue further nor must historians continue their work. After all, we already have such grand indoctrinative narratives – why continue to rewrite what has already been written? If, however, the purpose of history education is to develop one's ability to identify one's experience in a broader context, to establish one's sense of connection to the world, to develop intellectual competencies, skills, and dispositions necessary to be an independent, critical, and free-thinker in order to establish a sense of identity to a people or a place, then history educational practices must not stymie or obstruct the learning process by injecting politically-correct or indoctrinative measures that treat the study of the past like a restaurant buffet – where one can pick and choose as much or as little as one desires to satisfy one's monocular self-interests, personal convenience, and stagnant or void intellectualism. Hence, history education is not simply a phrase of subject, as its residual consequences have both built and destroyed empires. But why is history education so important in the Balkans and Kosovo in particular?

A recent declaration (Oct 22, 2013) by Turkish Prime Minister Erdogan proclaimed, in an outward show of historical and nationalistic new Ottoman rhetoric, "Kosovo is Turkey! Turkey is Kosovo![12] These inflammatory words ignited a backlash of political tension from Serbia toward Turkey, who also asserted, (especially since the 1999 occupation of NATO peacekeepers through the present), Kosovo is Serbia! Serbia is Kosovo! Both proclaim such rhetoric with good reason. After all, it was Serbia who, along with other peoples in the Balkans, led efforts to thwart Ottoman expansion in the 14th century. Moreover, it was at the so-called "Epic Battle of Kosovo Polje," on June 28, 1389, that the Serbian prince, Tsar Lazar and Ottoman Sultan Murat fought to the death to defend or claim the territory of what is now Kosovo. Tsar Lazar's resistance

---

[12] "Erdogan."

failed and the Ottoman Turks continued to push into the Balkans until approximately 70 years later, the Ottoman Sultans and Pashas governed the territory. Therefore, from a nationalistic standpoint, both countries' claim to the territory have, at least in one sense, historical legitimacy. But once again, the identity of those in the Balkans before Ottoman arrival and afterward is both or, in an unfortunate sense, one at the exclusion of other. In Ivo Andric's classic Nobel Peace Prize award-winning novel, *The Bridge on the Drina*, Andric presents the Balkans region of what is today's Bosnia from the perspective of a single bridge over a single river in a single village but of many peoples and languages over the course of four centuries.[13] Turk, Albanian, Serbian, Montenegrin, Christian, Muslim, Austro-Hungarian, priests, imams, herders, villagers, soldiers, lovers, merchants, Ottoman-appointed indigenous land governors, Pashas – all are represented in a manner that weaves, out of history a historical fiction, one of the best expositions of Balkan social and psychological identity. Honest and objective analysis of the Balkans will likely lead one to conclude that all parties' claims to the region are, in fact, predicated on foundations of truth. But what can one learn from all of this and, more importantly, where does history education fall among all of this?

---

[13] Andric, *The Bridge on the Drina*.

Transformative Education and Regional Identity

For Kosovo, the implementation of a quality public school history education program based *not* on nationalistic grand narratives, but one resting on a foundation of inquiry, has been in recurrent development by Kosovo's Ministry of Education, Science, and Technology (although stymied) for the past decade. After all, in this culturally rich landlocked Balkan nation, it has been ground-zero for many significant events and turning points in the region's history. But whose history is it? The aftermath of the 1999 Kosovo war and subsequent 2008 unilateral declaration of independence left Kosovo in an interesting position to reexamine its multicultural, nationalistic, and social history as it reforms itself from the poorest province in the former Yugoslavia to a modern democratic republic. In addition, despite its ethnic Albanian majority, political pressure from the European Union and the United States to establish and develop a functional multicultural society that fosters the rights and freedoms conducive to sustaining its democracy rest not only on its political, infrastructural, and business development, but a high quality educational institution that prepares its youth to make good on its commitment to sustain its democracy. To that end, the educational efforts to redefine history teaching to pedagogies fostering the knowledge, skills, and disposition necessary to develop and sustain a newborn democracy[14] is no small task and has been met with reluctance in many cases. At the issue's core is the problem of training knowledgeable teachers through institutional mission, vision, and goals that promote critical thinking, multiple perspectives, the use of sensitive and controversial issues, and a politically active citizenry to sustain the democracy. Currently, the teacher training institutions at the University of Pristina have little to offer in this area. In an attempt to address such an ambitious problem, forward-thinking Kosovar educators, the Council of Europe's Interculturalism and Bologna Process, a consortium of European partners invested in supporting the Kosovo Ministry of Education, Science, and Technology, published for free distribution, *History Teaching Today: Approaches and Methods[15]*, which provides a culmination of professional insights and pedagogical approaches for history teacher candidates and in-service history teachers to rebuild Kosovo's history education standards and practices to reflect modern international and disciplinary-congruence. *History Teaching Today: Approaches and Methods* is the culmination of six formal professional seminars sponsored by the Council of Europe and Interculturalism and Bologna Process with the Kosovo Ministry of Education, Science, and Technology intended to establish a working

---

[14] Franco, "Program Number 56112."
[15] Luisa Black, *History Teaching Today: Approaches and Methods*.

relationship and professional dialogue on the redevelopment of Kosovo's public school history teacher education program. The group's intent was to present current international best history teaching practices, paradigm shifts, and call to question traditional nationalistic grand narrative approaches, and provide an easy-to-read guide walking the reader through a process to re-think 21st century education in the Balkans and Kosovo in particular.[16]

This renewed approach rejects the selective and monocultural perspective of an old system and is contrasted by the presentation of issues unique to modern globalization, changes in the professionalization of teaching, and the value multiple perspectives can have on making the "...concept of nation state as the core of history curricula...outdated."[17] Such a proposition carries an electric charge within the social psychology of the Balkans, and with it, potential backlash against such attempts to stimulate a paradigm shift in pedagogical thought and practice. In essence, a renewed push for redeveloping public school history teacher preparation must be presented in a coherent exposition of the problems, proposed solutions, and clear teacher-friendly examples for the initial and sustained development of Kosovo's teachers. By adopting modern history teaching best practices that unpacks the study of

---

[16] Ibid.
[17] Ibid.

history through immersion into the ontological problem-sets and skills specific to the discipline of history, teachers and students alike hone their skills in source analysis and interpretation, historical thinking skills, critical thinking, narrative, and expository writing. Moreover, special attention on developing one's multipleperspectivity as a means to stimulate one's ability toward how to think rather than simply what to think is one means to wrestle with the rich multicultural mosaic within Kosovo and the Balkans in particular. To that end, when applying and presenting different interpretations of the past in history teaching, the impact on student learning can be enlightening toward the development of their own critical thinking and, in consequence, a more "…tolerant attitude towards different interpretations." [18]

Given the sensitivity of Kosovo's recent history, the issue of teaching history through the examination of multiple perspectives deserves special attention. By comparing the limited scope of monoperspectivity against a broader view of multipleperspectivity, history teachers in the Balkans must deal with a culture and familial oral traditions, myth-as-history, an the forementioned nationalistically-centered grand narratives. To facilitate this ambitious and controversial subject, Balkan history teachers are beginning to acknowledge the traditional

---

[18] Ibid.

monoperspective approach in the Balkans as "one-sided history – the nationalist history…" as "manipulation."[19] Kosovo's challenges on this point stem from the culturally-exclusive narratives which have divided the region's identity predicated on the Kosovo-Albanian, Kosovo-Serbian, Roma, Ashkali, Egyptian, Muslim, Catholic, Orthodox, and other ethnic perspectives and narratives. The core question is, *what historical narratives might result from consideration of all of such perspectives in redefining Kosovo's national identity?* Particular and careful attention to the point that multipleperspectivity is *not* relativism and must be underscored as such because through the careful use of rational argument, criteria grounded ethical elements, and historical analysis allow one to understand past's complexities. Moreover, the systematic tools of the historian such as source interpretation, factually centered objectivity, chronological understanding, causality, change and continuity, empathy, and inductive reasoning all promote the broadened perspectives that are conducive to healthy pluralistic societies.

As Kosovo continues on its trajectory as a new and stable democracy, she must educate her young citizens to take ownership in public affairs at the state and local level. To accomplish this, history education must provide students with the intellectual tools necessary to foster civic engagement,

---

[19] Ibid.

appreciation for social pluralism, and a tolerance for others predicated on the respect toward rule-of-law, equality, and multiple identities peacefully coexisting.[20] Such ideas are not new for Kosovo, but recent political challenges and a stagnating teacher education program presents significant challenges that complicate such reform endeavours. Effective and up-to-date history-teaching practices have much to offer toward empowering Kosovo's educational system into the 21st Century. But how can a renewed public school history education program assist in not only establishing regional identity in the Balkans, but also lead to regional stability? It seems overly simplistic to assume history education provides a proverbial "silver bullet" to a region with such a tumultuous past and multicultural complexities as the Balkans. After all, the quest for such stability has been a concern for members of the international community such as the United Nations, European Union, United States,[21] Russia, and does not seem to be on a trajectory for regional reconciliation. However, one must also consider this: what social forces lead to identity and stability in *any* region?

---

[20] OSCE, *Human Rights, Ethnic Relations and Democracy in Kosovo*.

[21] Woehrel, *Kosovo: Current Issues and U.S. Policy*, May 7, 2013; Woehrel, *Kosovo: Current Issues and U.S. Policy*, March 9, 2011.

[21] Sommers and Buckland, *Parallel Worlds: Rebuilding the Education System in Kosovo*.

Using inquiry-driven historical pedagogies dependent on close reading of primary sources married to the commitment to analyze sources not to support what one already believes to be true, but rather, to attain new knowledge of deeper understanding is the first step to establish a sense of place and its peoples. The development of a pan-regional identity rests on the commitment to view the Balkans not as a disparate set of peoples, despite a shared history – for better or worse. Even though the United States has 50 separate political sovereign in its Union, all with separate histories, the commitment to establish and agree upon a complex history which has, at times, been inspiring and, at worse, been shameful. But regional history does not have to establish isolated identities nor does it have to be exclusive or at the expense of another. For the United States, acknowledging its successes and ills are inherent to its regional or national memory. What then, is the pan-Balkan memory? How might the successes, ills, and complex sociopolitical events lend themselves to establishing a legitimate and regional memory? Instead of studying history in isolation in the Balkans, the opportunity exists for history education teachers and scholars to establish and develop a tradition of understanding the intense and tumultuous Balkan past while, at the same time, celebrating its unique culture not as was required under the old Yugoslavian system, not under systems of parallel structures,[22] and not of a singular national narrative. For the Balkans' story is an incomplete story without the inclusion of *all* its cast of characters; its controversial nationalistic politics; its several centuries of foreign occupation and rule; its internal tensions, wars, ethnic violence, blood feuds, and renewed push for alignment to modern industrial economic systems. A quality history education program allows students to examine all these things in light of their own personal and familial histories, to see where they fit into the pan-Balkan narrative and to learn from the past in order to understand the development, continuity, and change within the region. Such reflects the potential for history education's potential to have a transformative effect on one's view of the region's past. The challenge is whether or not the politicians, education policymakers and their interlocutors will promote such a radical proposition.

The use of the region's rich primary sources and well-trained history teachers committed to developing quality history curricula that maintains the discipline's integrity while, at the same time, creating learning environments facilitating high levels of student engagement presents significant substantive potential for the development of Kosovo's multicultural national identity as well as other nations in the region. On a much broader scale, such a history education program in Kosovo would constitute a *bleeding edge* initiative for sustaining its new democracy well into the 21st century. In its current state, Kosovo's history education, more as pro forma, is but a remnant of the Yugoslavian system at best, or a polarizing and exclusive ethno-nationalistic narrative centered on high levels of pro-Serbian or pan-Albanianism. Developing a regional history program predicated on source objectivity, critical thinking, multiple primary source material, source analysis, synthesis, promoting social voice and multiple perspectives has the potential for Kosovo to lead the Balkans at developing a *pan-Balkan identity* sans politically motivated and nationalistically exclusive grand narratives. Moreover, the development and establishment of such practices may lead history educators and scholars alike to *rethink* the meaning of the term, *Balkanization*. Modern best history teaching practices promoting students' construction of knowledge through historical method have the potential to make sweeping changes in the regional identity of the Balkans. Rather than its present connotation of extreme divisiveness, *Balkanization* could be transformed into a renewed meaning of reconciliation and 21st century regional identity.

Extended Bibliography

Ahtisaari, Marti. "Letter Dated 26 March 2007 from the Secretary-General Addressed to the President of the Security Council Addendum Comprehensive Proposal for the Kosovo Status Settlement." United Nations Security Council, March 26, 2007.

Andric, Ivo. *The Bridge on the Drina*. Translated by Lovett F. Edwards. Belgrade: Dereta, 2010.

Annea Hapciu, and John R. Sparks. *Kosovars: On Life in Kosovo*. Pristina, Kosovo: Frederich Ebert Foundation, October 2012.

———. *The Internal Effect of the Kosovo: The Young Europeans Nation Branding Campaign on the Kosovar People*. Pristina, Kosovo: Friedrich Ebert Foundation, October 2012.

Ball, Laurie. "United States Diplomacy in Kosovo Final Status Talks: A Case Study in Multilateral Negotiations With Principal Mediators." Master's Thesis, Princeton University, 2009. http://wws.princeton.edu/research/cases.xml.

Bilefsky, Dan. "Kosovo Declares Its Independence From Serbia." *The New York Times*. February 18, 2008. http://www.nytimes.com/2008/02/18/world/europe/18kosovo.html?pagewant ed=all.

———. "Kosovo Declares Its Independence From Serbia." *The New York Times*, February 18, 2008, sec. International / Europe. http://www.nytimes.com/2008/02/18/world/europe/18kosovo.html.

———. "Violence Mars Election in Kosovo." *The New York Times*, November 4, 2013, sec. World / Europe. http://www.nytimes.com/2013/11/05/world/europe/violence-mars-election-in-kosovo.html.

Bing, Bing. "The Independence of Kosovo: A Unique Case of Secession?" *Chinese Journal of International Law* 8, no. 1 (n.d.): 27–46. doi:10.109.

Bouas, George Arvanitis. "Peacekeeping in Kosovo." *TransConflict*. Accessed November 8, 2013. http://www.transconflict.com/2009/09/peacekeeping-in-kosovo/.

Bytyqi, Arlind V. "Nationalism and State Creation: The Kosovar Case." News and Media Portal about Kosova and the Balkans, February 3, 2008. www.Newkosovareport.com.

Colucci, Lamont. *The National Security Doctrines of the American Presidency: How They Shape Our Present and Future*. Vol. Two. First. Oxford, England: Praeger, 2012.

COMMISSION STAFF WORKING DOCUMENT KOSOVO* 2013 PROGRESS REPORT Accompanying the Document COMMUNICATION FROM THE COMMISSION TO THE EUROPEAN PARLIAMENT AND THE COUNCIL Enlargement Strategy and Main Challenges 2013-2014.

Brussels: European Commission, n.d.
ec.europa.eu/enlargement/pdf/key_documents/2013/.../kosovo_2013.pdf.

"Committee on Kosovo Calls for Unity, High Turnout - B92 English." *B92*.
Accessed November 8, 2013.
http://www.b92.net/eng/news/politics.php?yyyy=2013&mm=11&dd=07&na
v_id=88273.

Daalder, Ivo H., and Michael E. O'Hanlon. "The United States in the
Balkans: There to Stay." *The Washington Quarterly* 23, no. 4 (Autumn
2000): 157–170.

Dietrich, Frank. "The Status of Kosovo Reflections on the Legitimacy of
Secession." *Ethics & Global Politics* 3, no. 2 (2010): 123–142.
doi:10.3402/egp.v3i2.1983.

Durham, M. Edith. *High Albania*. Illustrated Edition. Middlesex: Echo
Library, 1909.

Dzihic, Vedran, and Helmut Kramer. *Kosovo After Independence: Is the
EU's EULEX Mission Delivering on It's Promises?* Berlin: International
Policy Analysis, July 2009.

Early Warning Report. Political and institutional stability Economic and
social stability Inter-ethnic relations Public and personal security, March
2007.

"Erdogan: 'Kosovo Is Turkey' - Al-Monitor: The Pulse of the Middle East."
Al-Monitor, January 22, 2013. http://www.al-
monitor.com/pulseen/originals/2013/10/erdogan-kosovo-turkey.html.

Fish, M. Steven. "Postcommunist Subversion: Social Science and
Democratization in East Europe and Eurasia." *Slavic Review* 58, no. 4
(Winter 1999): 794–823.

Fox, Dr Liam. "Europe Is Failing to Pull Its Weight in Nato."
Telegraph.co.uk, 19:54, sec. uknews.
http://www.telegraph.co.uk/news/uknews/defence/10518264/Europe-is-
failing-to-pull-its-weight-in-Nato.html.

Franco, Eric. "Thinking Like a Historian USAID Basic Education Program
History Teacher Workshop." History Teacher Workshop, Kosovo Ministry
of Education, Science, and Technology, Pristina, Kosovo, June 29, 2012.

Gallucci, Gerard. "Fear and Loathing in Kosovo." *TransConflict*. Accessed November 8, 2013. http://www.transconflict.com/2013/05/fear-and-loathing-in-kosovo-175/.

———. "Fundamentalists Take US Hostage." *TransConflict*. Accessed November 8, 2013. http://www.transconflict.com/2013/10/fundamentalists-take-us-hostage-810/.

———. "Kosovo - Conflict or Politics?" *TransConflict*. Accessed November 8, 2013. http://www.transconflict.com/2013/09/kosovo-conflict-or-politics-249/.

———. "Kosovo - the UN Role in the North." *TransConflict*. Accessed November 8, 2013. http://www.transconflict.com/2012/12/kosovo-the-un-role-in-the-north-172/.

———. "Kosovo - What If the Election Fails?" *TransConflict*. Accessed November 8, 2013. http://www.transconflict.com/2013/10/kosovo-election-fails-311/.

———. "Kosovo - What Next?" *TransConflict*. Accessed November 8, 2013. http://www.transconflict.com/2013/11/kosovo-what-next-711/.

———. "Kosovo - What or Who Can Convince the Northern Kosovo Serbs?" *TransConflict*. Accessed November 8, 2013. http://www.transconflict.com/2013/07/kosovo-what-or-who-can-convince-the-northern-kosovo-serbs-157/.

———. "Kosovo - What Role Will US Combat Troops Play in the North?" *TransConflict*. Accessed November 8, 2013. http://www.transconflict.com/2013/05/kosovo-what-role-will-us-combat-troops-play-in-the-north-275/.

———. "Kosovo - Who Gets to Decide EULEX's Departure?" *TransConflict*. Accessed November 8, 2013. http://www.transconflict.com/2013/07/kosovo-who-gets-to-decide-eulex-departure-297/.

———. "Kosovo – Partitioning What from What?" *TransConflict*. Accessed November 8, 2013. http://www.transconflict.com/2009/12/kosovo-partitioning-what-from-what/.

———. "Kosovo – What Is to Be Done?" *TransConflict*. Accessed November 8, 2013. http://www.transconflict.com/2009/11/kosovo-what-is-to-be-done/.

————. "Kosovo and the Ahtisaari Plan." *TransConflict*. Accessed November 8, 2013. http://www.transconflict.com/2009/09/kosovo-and-the-ahtisaari-plan/.

————. "The Ahtisaari Plan and North Kosovo." *TransConflict*. Accessed November 8, 2013. http://www.transconflict.com/approach/think/policy/ahtisaari-plan-north-kosovo/.

————. "Time for the UN Security Council Permanent Five to Give up Their Vetoes?" *TransConflict*. Accessed November 8, 2013. http://www.transconflict.com/2013/06/time-for-the-un-security-council-permanent-five-to-give-up-their-vetoes-126/.

————. "US Foreign Policy and the Pursuit of 'democracy.'" *TransConflict*. Accessed November 8, 2013. http://www.transconflict.com/2013/07/us-foreign-policy-and-the-pursuit-of-democracy-087/.

————. "What Is Belgrade Doing with Kosovo?" *TransConflict*. Accessed November 8, 2013. http://www.transconflict.com/2013/09/belgrade-kosovo-189/.

Garcia-Orrico, Debra. *United Nations Security Council Resolutions Under Chapter VII (Kosovo)*, n.d.

Gender-Based Violence in Kosovo: A Case Study. Pristina, Kosovo: United Nations Population Fund, July 2005.

General Charles Krulak. "The Strategic Corporal: Leadership in the Three Block War." *Marines Magazine*, January 1999. http://www.google.com/url?sa=t&rct=j&q=&esrc=s&frm=1&source=web&cd=4&cad=rja&ved=0CEMQFjAD&url=http%3A%2F%2Fwww.dtic.mil%2Fcgi-bin%2FGetTRDoc%3FAD%3DADA399413&ei=oieKUruAK-KQyQGT_4HYCQ&usg=AFQjCNEgzAIz4CSA9UT9EeUjh4pgD96J_A.

Gjcov, Shtjefen, and Leonard Fox. *The Code of Leke Dukagjini*. New York, New York: Gjonlekaj Publishing Company, 1989.

Glenny, Misha. *The Balkans: Nationalism, War, and the Great Powers, 1804-1999*. New York, New York: Viking, 2000.

Goodin, Robert E., and Charles Tilly, eds. *The Oxford Handbook of Contextual Political Analysis*. Oxford, England: Oxford University Press, 2006.

Herbert, Matthew Wood. "Who Deserves Kosovo? An Argument from Social Contract Theory." *Southeast European Politics* VI, no. 1 (July 2005): 29–43.

"Is Serbia Concealing Its Agenda on Kosovo? :: Balkan Insight." Accessed November 8, 2013. http://www.balkaninsight.com/en/article/is-serbia-concealing-its-agenda-on-kosovo.

"Is Turkey Being Excluded From the Middle East Equation? - Al-Monitor: The Pulse of the Middle East." *Al-Monitor*. Accessed January 24, 2014. http://www.al-monitor.com/pulseen/politics/2013/10/turkey-exclusion-mideast-equation-fidan.html.

Jeton Musliu. "Kosovo Textbooks Soften Line on Ottoman Rule." BIRN -- Balkan Insight. *Kosovo Textbooks Soften Line on Ottoman Rule*, January 22, 2013. http://www.balkaninsight.com/en/article/kosovo-textbooks-soften-line-on-ottoman.

Judah, Tim. *Kosovo: What Everyone Needs to Know*. Oxford: Oxford University Press, 2008.

———. *The Serbs: History, Myth and the Destruction of Yugoslavia*. 3rd ed. London: Yale University Press, 2010.

Katulis, Brian. "U.S. Diplomacy Toward Kosovo: 1989-1999." Master's Thesis, Princeton University, 2000. http://wws.princeton.edu/research/cases.xml.

Ker-Lindsay, James. *Kosovo: The Path to Contested Statehood in the Balkans*. New York, New York: I.B. Tauris, 2009.

Krulak, General Charles. Marine Corps General Charles Krulak on the US intervention in Kosovo, 1999. PBS Frontline Website: War in Europe. Accessed November 18, 2013. http://www.pbs.org/wgbh/pages/frontline/shows/kosovo/interviews/krulak.html.

Kugler, Richard L., and Marianna Kozinsteva. *Enlarging NATO: The Russia Factor*. Santa Monica, California: RAND, 1996.

Luisa Black. *History Teaching Today: Approaches and Methods*. Brussels: Council of Europe, May 2011.

Mackey, Produced By Robert, Beth Flynn Photos, and Narration By Andrew Testa. "Photographer's Journal: Kosovo, Year 1." *The New York Times*, February 17, 2009, sec. International / Europe. http://www.nytimes.com/interactive/2009/02/17/world/europe/20090217-kosovo-anniversary/index.html.

Macshane, Denis. *Why Kosovo Still Matters*. London: Haus Publishing LTD., 2011.

Magalachvili, Denis. "Kosovo: A Critique of a Failed Mission." *Mediterranean Quarterly* 16, no. 3 (Summer 2005): 118–141.

Malcolm, Noel. *Kosovo: A Short History*. Washington Square, New York: New York university Press, 1998.

Meyer, Steven. "Security Council Resolution 1244 - Everyone's Favorite Crutch." *TransConflict*, March 2013. http://www.transconflict.com/2013/03/security-council-resolution-1244-everyones-favorite-crutch-113/.

Miller, Benjamin, and Korina Kagan. "The Great Powers and Regional Conflicts: Eastern Europe and the Balkans from Post-Nepoleonic Era to the Post-Cold War Era." *International Studies Quarterly* 41, no. 1 (March 1997): 51–85.

Milosevic, Slobodan. "SLOBODAN MILOSEVIC'S 1989 ST. VITUS DAY SPEECH," June 28, 1989. http://cmes.arizona.edu/sites/cmes.arizona.edu/files/SLOBODAN%20MILOSEVIC_speech_6_28_89.pdf.

Moisi, Dominique. "Turkey's Lost Illusions." *Project Syndicate*, October 24, 2013. http://www.project-syndicate.org/commentary/dominique-moision-the-marginalization-of-the-middle-east-s-key-player/english.

Musliu, Jeton. "Kosovo Textbooks Soften Line on Ottoman Rule :: Balkan Insight." January 22, 2013. *Kosovo Textbooks Soften Line on Ottoman Rule*. Accessed January 25, 2014. http://www.balkaninsight.com/en/article/kosovo-textbooks-soften-line-on-ottoman.

"NATO, EU Secure Polling Stations in Vote Re-Run Central to Kosovo Accord." *Yahoo News*. Accessed November 18, 2013. http://news.yahoo.com/nato-eu-secure-polling-stations-vote-run-central-095642245.html.

"News Hour with Jim Lehrer." Online, Internet. *Online News Hour*. PBS, June 25, 1999. http://www.pbs.org/newshour/bb/military/jan-june99/krulak_6-25.html.

O'Neill, William G. *Kosovo: An Unfinished Peace*. London: Lynne Rienner Publishers, 2002.

Obradovic, Jelena. *Kosovo: A View From Serbia*. Security Studies. Paris: European Union Institute for Security Studies, April 2008.

OSCE. *Human Rights, Ethnic Relations and Democracy in Kosovo*. Background Report. Pristina, Kosovo: Organization for Security and Co-operation in Europe OSCE Mission in Kosovo, Summer -Summer 2008 2007.

Pashoja-Myftiu, Ganimete. *Refugees in New H(e)aven*. 1st ed. Pristina, Kosovo: Kosova, 2002.

"PBS Frontline: War in Europe." Streaming -- Online. *FROL1811*. A WGBH/FRONTLINE and Channel 4 coproduction in association with Mentorn Barraclough Carey and Kirk Documentary Group, Ltd. Copyright 2000 WGBH EDUCATIONAL FOUNDATION ALL RIGHTS RESERVED, February 22, 2000. PBS Frontline: http://www.pbs.org/wgbh/pages/frontline/shows/kosovo/. http://www.pbs.org/wgbh/pages/frontline/shows/kosovo/.

Peci, Edona. "Albania Independence Day Fervour Still Grips Kosovo :: Balkan Insight." BIRN. *Balkan Insight*, November 28, 2013. http://www.balkaninsight.com/en/article/albania-independence-day-fervour-still-grips-kosovo.

Petrov, Vladimir. "'Independence' for Kosovo or a Domino Effect?" *International Affairs* 52, no. 3 (2006): 76–84.

Pevehouse, Jon C., and Joshua S. Goldstein. "Serbian Compliance or Defiance in Kosovo? Statistical Analysis and Real-Time Predictions." *The Journal of Conflict Resoluton* 43, no. 4 (August 1999): 538–546.

Philips, John. *Macedonia: Warlords & Rebels in the Balkans*. London: I.B. Tauris, 2004.

Pond, Elizabeth. "Kosovo: Catalyst for Europe." *Washington Quarterly* 22, no. 4 (Autimn 1999): 77–92.

Property Return and Restitution: Kosovo Prepared for Review of Covenant Law Issues in Kosovo by the UN Committee on Economic, Social and Cultural Rights. United Nations. Pristina, Kosovo: United Nations Centre on Housing Rights and Evictions, March 31, 2008.

Pula, Besnik. "The Emergence of the Kosovo 'Parallel State,' 1988-1992." *Nationalities Papers* 32, no. 4 (December 2004): 797–826.

Roth, Guenther. "Personal Rulership, Patrimonialism, and Empire-Building in the New States." *World Politics* 20, no. 2 (January 1968): 194–206.

Sackur, Stephen. "BBC HardTalk." *BBC HARDtalk*, September 1, 2010. http://www.youtube.com/watch?v=xebqdjYnLZ4; http://www.youtube.com/watch?v=DmJl4pBsIlw.

———. "BBC HARDtalk." *Mimoza Kusari-Lila - Deputy PM and Minister of Trade & Industry, Kosovo*. BBC, April 8, 2013. http://www.youtube.com/watch?v=BHNgU_rffb0.

Sommers, Marc, and Peter Buckland. *Parallel Worlds: Rebuilding the Education System in Kosovo*. Working Document. Paris: International Institute for Educational Planning (UNESCO), 2004.

Steven Woehrel. *Kosovo's Independence and U.S. Policy*. Congressional Report. CRS Report for Congress. Washington, D.C.: Congressional Research Service, July 22, 2008.

Surroi, Veton. *The Book of Butterflies*. 1st ed. Pristina, Kosovo: Koha, 2013.

The Helsinki Moment: European Member-State Building in the Balkans. Executive Summary. Berlin-Brussels-Istanbul: European Stability Initiative, February 1, 2005.

The Lausanne Principle: Multiethnicity, Territiry, and the Future of Kosovo's Serbs. Berlin/Pristina: European Stability Initiative, June 7, 2004.

The Western Balkans: Moving on. Chaillot Paper. Paris: Institute for Security Studies, October 2004.

Tole, Vasil S. *Encyclopedia of Albanian Folk Iso-Polyphony*. Tirana, Albania: Shtepia Botuese Uegen, 2007.

Troebst, Stefan. *Conflict in Kosovo -- Failure of Prevention An Analytical Documentation, 1992-1998*. Working Paper. Flensburg, Germany: European Centre for Minority Issues, May 1998.

"United Nations Security Council Resolution 1244." United Nations Security Council, June 10, 1999.

"Vote in Kosovska Mitrovica on November 17 - B92 English." *B92.* Accessed November 8, 2013. http://www.b92.net/eng/news/politics.php?yyyy=2013&mm=11&dd=07&nav_id=88261.

Woehrel, Steven. *Future of the Balkans and U.S. Policy Concerns.* Congressional Report. Washington, D.C.: Congressional Research Service, January 18, 2006.

————. *Future of the Balkans and U.S. Policy Concerns.* Congressional Report. CRS Report for Congress. Washington, D.C.: Congressional Research Service, January 10, 2008.

————. *Kosovo: Current Issues and U.S. Policy.* Congressional Report. CRS Report for Congress. Washington, D.C.: Congressional Research Service, May 7, 2013.

————. *Kosovo: Current Issues and U.S. Policy.* CRS Report for Congress. Washington, D.C.: Congressional Research Service, March 9, 2011.

————. *Kosovo's Future Status and U.S. Policy.* Congressional Report. Congressional Research Service, January 9, 2006.
Zefi, Shan. *Islamiazation of Albanians Through Centuries.* 1st. ed. Prizren,

Kosovo: Drita, 2006

Kosovo in Transition: The Search for a Modern Identity

Ally Whittaker

WHEN war broke out in Kosovo in 1998, I was seven years old. While ethnic tension and acts of violence escalated half way around the world from me, I was in school trying to memorize the poem "Flanders Field" to recite on Remembrance Day. I had never seen a real poppy, but the poem gave me the impression that the flowers grew where people had died fighting for the freedom of their country. In Kosovo, the poppies grow in abundance. In fact, they grow everywhere; springing up through the cracks in the pavement, filling open fields, appearing here and there even in the cities. I thought they were beautiful, but the Kosovars call them weeds. They do not like to talk about the war that raged through the region only 14 years ago. It has been argued that the tensions in Kosovo began as a pursuit for a national identity, with Albanians asserting that Kosovo was rightfully their nation, while Serbians insisted that as a province of Serbia, the land was a part of their own heritage. Despite the tremendous changes to the now independent country of Kosovo, and the accelerated modernization the area has undergone since the war, it seems that the original pursuit of a collective identity continues to challenge the Albanian nation to this day.

Kosovo declared independence in 2008, having been a province of Serbia since the break-up of Former Yugoslavia until the war in 1999, after which the area was governed under UNMIK for nearly 10 years. I was given an incredible opportunity to live in Kosovo for a brief time to study post conflict resolution in this interesting and turbulent region. The Balkans Peace Program, hosted by the Bislimi Group Foundation, brought students from around the world to participate in a 3 week university course, and paired us with host families for the duration of our stay. Our group consisted of students from Alberta, Ontario, London, and Prague. The class was a seminar style discussion involving both international and local students, which provided a more well-rounded discussion with multiple perspectives. Moreover, living with a host family immersed us in the local culture completely, which became a learning experience in itself. My host was an ambitious and enthusiastic seventeen-year old. She greeted me from the airport bouncing on her feet and telling me she couldn't sleep all night, she had been so excited trying to make everything perfect for my visit. While she was not particularly confident in her English on the first day, by the end of my stay we were chatting constantly;

not only was she fluent in English, but she was incredibly helpful as an Albanian language instructor and translator for me as well. The program was not comprised only of the seminar class, but included visits to Pristina, the capital of Kosovo, to meet with various government officials. During our final week in Kosovo, we took a 5 day road trip spanning Montenegro, Albania, and Macedonia, to see the sights and learn about the history of the region. This paper aims to document what I learned about Kosovo through the experiences I have had in this young country.

Part One: Conflict in Kosovo and the Creation of a Cultural Memory

Throughout the 19th and 20th centuries, nationalism and self-definition have been utilized as ideological tools for bolstering public and political identities across many nations, mainly originating in Western Europe. Kosovo has always contained a pluralistic society comprising many ethnic and religious backgrounds; from Albanians, Serbians and Turks, to Muslims and Catholics. It stands to reason that Kosovo has thus been a place of a multitude of competing narratives of different ethnic and national identities. Due to a constant flow of migration, violence, and political schemes throughout history, Kosovo lacked control over its own independence, while Empires rose and dissolved around it (Buckley & Cummings, 2001, p. 13). A collective sense of identity will also typically draw a distinct line between the self, and 'the other'. Recently in Kosovo, this 'other' has been formed on terms of ethnic differences, mainly between Albanians and Serbians. Of course, ethnic Serbians and Albanians both do not fit fully into the state boundaries that have been set out on our global maps, resulting in a large diaspora of both groups, many of which call Kosovo their rightful home. A trend of ethnic separation grew from the 1980's through the 1990's, so that Albanians were separated from Serbians, as all ethnic groups lived in their own villages or neighbourhoods (Judah, 2008, p. 4-5). The open hostility and common violence between Albanians and Serbians in Kosovo has been cyclical over the years; Albanians may have treated Serbians wrongly in the past and in the aftermath of the war, while the Serbians committed atrocities against Albanians leading up to and during the war (Buckley & Cummings, 2001, p. 33). This intensified as conflicts between the Serbians and Albanians grew stronger.

Kosovo today has a population of about two million. Of that, nearly 90% is Albanian, while less than 10% is mainly Serbian. By the end of the war, it is estimated that 800 000 Albanian Kosovars had left the region, either by force or fleeing the violence, while up to 400 000 had been internally displaced within Kosovo. Moreover, about 7 000 ethnic Albanians were killed as a result of the open hostility, both from the Serbian violence as well as the NATO bombings (Buckley & Cummings, 2001, p. 1, 23). The bulk of the Albanian Kosovar refugees returned to the region quite quickly following the war, although a large diaspora spans across Western Europe and North America as well. It is interesting to note that Albanian people, as a nation, are held together by language, whereas Serbians typically define themselves by being Orthodox (Judah, 2008). There is little reconciliation to this day between Albanians and Serbians, leaving the society in stagnation, unwilling to return to a time of such violent ethnic hatred, yet also finding it difficult to set aside generations of antagonism and a history of alternating suppression. Although there are two official languages in Kosovo, Albanian and Serbian, the younger members of the population rarely know both, opting instead to study English as their second language, and the common language through which the two groups can communicate. Serbians have always considered Kosovo to be an important part of their heritage dating back centuries, and as such, they regard the independence of Kosovo and its Albanian majority as a blow to their own cultural identity. Many Albanians, on the other hand, wish to become a province of Albania. The Albanian often flag flies next to the Kosovo flag, and a quick Google search will show that many casual, non-scholarly sources will place Pristina within Kosovo, Albania, as if Kosovo already is a province of Albania. Even when I was explaining to others back home where I was going, I had to tell them I was going to Albania; they did not know where Kosovo was. Yet it became clear during my travels that the iron curtain that separated Kosovo and Albania during the Cold War had an effect on both societies' development. Kosovo has a more youthful and vibrant atmosphere, while Albania feels older and more moderate. The Albanian dialects also grew quite differently, so that Kosovo Albanian sounds like a slang version of proper Albanian. As well as being politically separated, Kosovar Albanians were physically and culturally separated from Albania by the strict Serbian rule leading up to the war.

NATO intervened in Kosovo after violence had escalated to the events in Racak, in which Serbians massacred nearly 50 civilian Albanians thought to have been associated with the Kosovo Liberation Army. Seventy-eight days of NATO bombing followed this episode, killing many people on both sides, including civilians (Buckley & Cummings, 2001, p. 21). This intervention was a conscious decision by NATO to supersede the ruling of the UN Security Council, in which Russia had vetoed international interference in Kosovo. Later as trial was held in which it was ultimately decided that although it was illegal for NATO to intervene without permission, their action had been just. The violence in the region had escalated to a point which the international community took as an implication that

Milosevic had entirely disregarded the protection of human rights for Albanian Kosovars. Moreover, evidence of mass graves being constructed was found after the war was over, implying that the war ended before the worst of it could occur (Judah, 2008, p. 87-90). Although the NATO bombings caused many deaths itself, the intervention likely ended the war much sooner than it would have concluded on its own.

The NATO intervention is often celebrated, especially by Americans, for preventing a similar situation to that in Bosnia only a few years earlier, which had created a feeling of guilt within the international community for their unwillingness to step in. Many studies cite this guilt as one of the primary reasons for NATO taking action when they did, and for the less severe punishment they received afterwards. Post-Cold War globalization and the nature of today's wars involve "a myriad of transnational connections so that the distinction between internal and external... between local and global, are difficult to maintain" (Moore, 2001, p. 73). As such, in the fourteen years following the war, the world has been discussing the implications of what happened in Kosovo and how it will affect previously Westphalian concepts of nation-state sovereignty. The situation brings up questions of whether or not Kosovo should be considered the new precedent for foreign relations, or if this type of intervention should be an exception to the standard rules, but only if absolutely necessary. Debates have surrounded the sort of commitment that international organizations such as NATO, the EU, and the UN should have towards the citizens that make up their components (Buckley & Cummings, 2001, p. 2009). The Ahtisaari Plan was developed in the peace talks following the war. It allowed a supervised independence for a multi-ethnic Kosovo, with an Albanian majority, although Serbians and other ethnicities are given substantive autonomy within their own communities. It also called for a strong international presence to maintain peace and repel conflict. For better or worse, the aftermath of Kosovo called for a re-organization of international relations in Europe and America, NATO, and the UN, as well as redefined the international community as a defender of all Human Rights. (Buckley & Cummings, 2001, p. 219)

It was interesting to note that Kosovo is one of the few places I have travelled in Europe where the locals are typically quite enthusiastic to have Americans visit. Even when I insisted that I am actually a Canadian, they did not often distinguish the two countries. This is fair enough, as I am well aware that many people in North America do not differentiate between 'Kosovo' and 'the Balkans', either. The reason Kosovars consider Americans so admirable is because the Western power has been a significant political ally on Kosovo's road to independence. America showed tremendous support for Kosovo in the arena of international politics as it negotiated with the EU and the UN for sovereignty and a place in the international community, and officially recognized the nation soon after they had declared themselves independent in 2008. As well, America has continued to encourage other nations to also recognize Kosovo's independent status. Of course not all of Kosovar society feels the same way, but typically, I found that ties to America area well-respected source of pride.

Despite the conversation that the rest of the world continues to hold, regarding Kosovo as a strong case supporting the need for a global security system, the local population in Kosovo does not like to discuss the war very often. Although the violence between Kosovar Albanians and Kosovar Serbs has not been completely eradicated, hostility between the two groups has significantly decreased in this region since the war. One older man that I questioned explained to me why grudges against entire ethnicities cannot be upheld; he told me, "I have Serbian neighbours; they are part of my community. What is done is over. If I forgive no one, how will I find peace? No, I cannot blame them for what happened to all of us". My fellow international students and I repeatedly attempted to initiate conversations on what Kosovo was like decade and a half ago, but outside of the classrooms we were usually met with vague answers and an abrupt change of topic. Luckily, our travels included visits to museums and historical sights, giving us plenty of opportunity to ask questions and to learn about the events surrounding the aforementioned war. It was good to see that memorials and centers for learning existed, despite the peoples reluctance to discuss the past. As a history major, I value institutions with a mission to preserve and to propagate a nation's heritage, although it is important to understand the subjective nature of such institutions, as their aim is usually to express the identity that they have created.

Some of the sights we visited were dedicated to Albanian culture or Kosovo history from very long ago, while some were memorials to the recent war. We were even taken to locations of natural beauty, to see all that Kosovo had to offer visitors. For example, we drove through the country, winding around mountains, and walked along river trails up to a view of a stunning waterfall. Later we visited Prizren, an old fashioned and beautiful city, and we climbed to the top of a hill, where the ruins of a castle overlook the entire town. Likewise, the Shkodra castle ruins perch atop a grassy hill in Albania, which not only allowed for a wonderful unobstructed view upon the modern city of Shkodra, but the castle walls play a prominent role in many Albanian folktales. Similarly, the Gadime Cave is not only a physical attraction, but tells Kosovo history through the shapes and stories that can be found in the natural formation of

Stalagmites and Stalactites. We were told that one such formation used to look like an Eagle, but it was partially broken after the war. I wondered if it had represented an eagle before the NATO intervention as well, and if it really had been Serbian forces that broke it. Reverence for America's role in Kosovo's recent history was obvious in the Kosovo Museum we visited in Pristina, as well, with many news articles, images, and items documenting the 'atrocities committed by Serbs' and the celebration of NATO as saviours of the country. Interestingly, the floor below the war memorials held an archaeology exhibit, displaying items from centuries past. By layering historical time periods and tying objects on display to modern Kosovo, they re-enforce the idea of a long-standing Albanian identity in the region. The way in which history is represented can teach us just as much about the current culture of any given place as it teaches the historical events they are connected to.

Two places that we visited struck me particularly strongly, mainly due to the parallels that were drawn between the two cultural myths surrounding them. The first was the Skanderbeg museum, standing at the pinnacle of the medieval-style Albanian town of Kruja. The museum centered on Skanderbeg as an Albanian hero from the fifteenth century. He is mainly remembered as the leader of an Albanian resistance force against the Ottoman Empire's expansion into the Balkan region, although he later became an Albanian cultural symbol of cohesion, both among Albanians and with the rest of Europe (Fischer & Schwandner-Sievers, 2002, p. 43). This development was the beginning of an Albanian national consciousness which now spreads across the Albanian diaspora, including Kosovo. The second location, this time in Kosovo itself, is from a significantly more recent period of time; the Jashari memorial house in Prekaz. Adem Jashari and other family members were active leaders within the Kosovo Liberation Army, and in March of 1998, Serbian forces attacked the Albanian militants in their home. All but one was killed in the fight, and their graves are in a line near the house, which has remains preserved in its ruined state, the walls riddled with bullet holes and scorch marks (Judah, 2008, p. 81).The massacre of the Jashari family became something of a legend, and the family has been celebrated as martyrs for the Albanian cause, so much so that the house has been preserved in its ruined state and become a place of pilgrimage. Parallels are drawn between Skanderbeg and Adem Jashari to give the nation heroes whom they can rally around and use to help to form their sense of identity and pride. The formation of an identity based on an active resistance to 'the other', be it the Ottomans or the Serbians, is a common theme throughout history. For example, after Scotland had recently become a part of the United Kingdom, wars were being fought between the Monarchs of France and those of Britain, and so they needed to find a way to unite their divided regions to support their cause. As such, a new and inclusive British identity needed to be formed. They may have had little in common, but they could relate to one another by asserting that they were certainly not 'the French'. This creation of 'the other' helped to unite a nation against a common cause. Cultural myths are built up throughout history to solidify these identities, and the stories of Skanderbeg and Jashari have become the focus of a new identity of Kosovar Albanians, a 'founding myth' for their national identity.

Part Two: Kosovo Today and the Formation of a Modern Identity

Currently, Kosovo faces the challenge of bridging the gap between tradition and modernity. The country has all the signs of a transitioning society that is embracing change while trying to maintain some traditional social norms. The capital city, Pristina, shows off their pride for this new and modern Kosovo with giant letters in the middle of the city that say 'Newborn'. It is painted with flags of other countries as well as signatures and messages left by visitors, welcoming a globalized world. In many ways, Kosovo can be similar to Canada. They have all the amenities I see at home, nice cars and fancy restaurants, shopping malls and dance clubs, movie theatres and cafes. I was often asked if it was strange to live in a primarily Muslim society, but I have found that Albanians are generally quite secular. No rules were imposed upon me, people my age wore clothing similar to mine, and my host family welcomed open discussion on religion and multitude of other topics. The cultural differences between Canada and Kosovo were more noticeable in older generations, but that has more to do with traditional practices in society than it has to do with religion itself. As this new nation struggles to re-articulate a post-communist, post-war identity, their new sense of belonging becomes "superimposed" onto the former, traditional identity (Moore, 2001, p. 32).

Familial ties have always been deeply important to the Albanian society. Indeed, there was a time when the extended family provided the greatest, if not the only "safety net" possible in a place of violence and social upheaval (Moore, 2001, p. 36). In general, I noticed that family relationships were closer and more important to individuals in Kosovo than in Canada, at least in the case of my host family. Aside from my host, who was the youngest in the family, there were 3 other daughters, one who was married and lived in a nearby village, and two who still lived at home. Their grandmother also lives with them, and neighbours often came over to visit, so the house was always quite full. I rarely saw my host father, as he left for work before I was awake and he often came home late. He was quiet and kept to himself, but when he did speak English his accent was clear and easy to understand. My host mother spoke no English, but took great delight when I stumbled over Albanian pleasantries, such as 'hello,' (Përshëndetje), 'good morning' (miremengjesi) or 'thank you' (faleminderit) and 'very good' (shume mire!). The hospitality I experienced and the way I was completely accepted by my host family made me feel so much more comfortable for the duration of my time in Gjilan.

I was told that when my host-sisters were children, older generations preferred male children, and many comments were directed towards the family of how unfortunate it was for the parents that they had four girls and no sons. However, my host Father felt differently, and proudly exclaimed how delighted he was to have daughters. Of course, the younger generations viewpoints on family size and even on having children at all is radically different from countless generations preceding them, most of whom desired large, male dominated family structures. Traditional gender roles had long been an unquestioned aspect of society, and have only just begun to change in recent times. Most industries are male dominated, and only in the last decade has the ratio of women in post-secondary schooling become equal to men. Mothers were expected to stay at home and look after the family, while younger women have a more difficult time finding work than men. This is partially due to the belief on the part of employers that a job should be given to a man supporting a wife and children, before a woman who is only supporting herself or assisting the family. However, this does not take into account women who are supporting their families, rather than the men. Even now, when we visited the military base I noticed very few females, and those I did see were the young ones in training, no women were leading us around the base, answering our questions, translating between Albanian and English, or giving us presentations. In class we also acknowledged how, in post-war societies, gender equality becomes a difficult discussion. War creates a climate where mistreatment and crimes against women are abundant, yet in post war societies such as Kosovo, women are often reluctant to share their stories, making it difficult for them to heal or move on. It has only recently become socially acceptable to openly discuss matters such as rape, prostitution, trafficking, and violence in a public space, and even so, some members of society consider it a highly taboo topic now (Voorhoeve, 2007, p. 71-73). One incredible example of the perseverance of Kosovar women was during the war, in the village of Krusha e Madhe. In 1998, the Serbian forces killed all the men and boys who were capable of fighting, leaving only women, the elderly, and young children. The women of the village, instead of giving in to despair, instead began to produce a kind of jam. It grew so popular that it is now available in grocery stores in Kosovo, and is one of the countries more viable commodities to export. Rebuilding the village so it is once again economically successful is a true example of women being strong and resilient in the face of tragedy. Their success inspires hope in other Kosovar women; so much that women in the workplace and in universities has become rapidly more common. Now, 14 years after the war, Kosovo currently has a female president. Moreover, the young women whom I spent time with are intelligent and strong, with ambitious hopes and dreams. The gender gap is closing, albeit slowly.

On top of the question of gender, there is an obvious generational gap. Not only is Kosovo a young nation having been independent only since 2008, but about half of Kosovo's population in under the age of 25, allowing this young nation to be invigorating and modern. When we met with Hajdin Abazi, the Deputy Minister of Culture, Youth, and Sports, he agreed that this large, youthful population would be a challenge for the next few years, but he was optimistic about the future of Kosovo. I already mentioned that Young Kosovars dress just like the average Canadian youth, and that young Kosovo is mainly secular. Younger generations in Kosovo are less likely to adhere strictly to religious practices and traditional expectations of older members of society. Those who were only children during the war and grew up primarily in post-war Kosovo are less concerned with memories of the war, as they were quite young when it happened and they grew up in a culture not willing to talk about the events in great detail. They turn their thoughts to the future instead, worrying both about themselves, in terms of employment and travel, as well as the nation, in terms of politics and economics. The concept of globalization is welcomed by this generation, as they use the internet and travel, if they can, to learn about and interact with the rest of the world. Along that line, I have never met more avid Facebook users. The social media site has become its own culture among them; constantly updating photos of themselves, posting links to news and organizations, and sending messages to friends, family, and contacts around the world. Information spreads rapidly among this generation. In fact, one night in Montenegro as we were eating dinner by the ocean, as storm rolled in. It was dark, pouring rain, and the waves were growing taller, crashing on to the beach. Naturally, part of our group decided to go swimming in it! The coast guard kicked them off the beach for being unsafe, but not soon enough to avoid a large crowd of people taking photos and videos. By the time we returned to the hotel, the owner had Facebook photo's up on her phone and excitedly asked if they were of us. At the time, this constant connection to others via the internet seemed intense, but now that I am on the other side of the world it allows me to have up-to-date, personal information on what is happening in Kosovo, and with the people I met there. The way that this young nation embraces change and globalization is promising for Kosovo's future.

Perhaps it is my own strong sense of wanderlust, but I was constantly struck by the fact that many Kosovars cannot travel. It is very difficult to get a visa to visit countries outside of the Balkan region, and trips are thus limited to Macedonia or Albania, for example. Even if my travel was limited to Canada only, I could venture far and wide, but in Kosovo it only takes a few hours to drive from border to border. I was told by many different people that obtaining a travel visa is like winning the lottery, or finding the golden ticket to the chocolate factory. (Their pop culture references, by the way, are outstandingly better than mine. We only have to ask something along the lines of "what's that movie with the song and that guy?" and they will not only hastily tell us the English title, but also the names of all the main actors in it.) A large portion of Kosovar Albanians who do get to leave have migrated to other parts of Europe, Canada, and America. You can see this simply by observing flight patterns at the Pristina international airport. The most common flights are to Switzerland, Germany, and Austria. These are also popular holiday destinations for those who can go. My host wistfully told me of all the places in the world she wished o see, and I sincerely hope we will be able to have our new Kosovar friends come to study in Canada one day as well.

Kosovo is not only young, but quite poor by European standards. This is visible throughout the small nation, though not as clearly as one may expect. The main economic issue is the lack of employment. Statistics state that 45 percent of Kosovo's population is unemployed, although in reality this is probably higher, as I have been told that students and youth are not included in the unemployed category, even though they are also often searching for work. As we walked to and from class in the middle of the day, a disproportionate number of adults were sitting in coffee shops or on the streets, and there were many beggars even in the small town of Gjilan. We quickly experienced what we dubbed the 'café culture' in Kosovo; wherein entire days were spend jumping from one café to the next. We would sit in one and have a coffee, and go to the next place for a pizza, and another place for a cola, and that is often how we passed time during the day. We international students also spent some days travelling around to see the sights of Kosovo or attend meetings with politicians, but for those who live here and for whom there are no new sights to see in Kosovo, there is little else to do. Furthermore, both grandparents and adult children often live at home, not all of whom can find work, placing financial strain on the family. Due to the stagnated economic development, significantly more goods must be imported than can be exported. Some of the local students bragged about their food, and how they only ate traditional Albanian food in Kosovo. While it was true that almost all menus featured the same food, and much of it was traditional to the region, the most common foods were modern developments such as pizza and French fries. Italian food was also featured, often with Italian names as well-margarita pizza, spaghetti bolognese, or primavera; this is perhaps a relic of decades past, when Kosovo was under Italian control. Another boast was how healthy the food was. This is quite simply, and unfortunately not true. Despite the beautiful green landscape of rolling hills and valleys full of presumably fertile land, they simply lack the infrastructure to harvest natural resources. Instead, the majority of their food is imported, packaged and chemically preserved. With the exception of small fruit stands and bakery's that dot the streets of Gjilan and Pristina, the majority of the food in Kosovo is not fresh. The problem is not that the small country does not have resources, for they have a large base of unemployed workers and open land, among others, but that they lack the infrastructure to capitalize on and improve their exports.

Our meeting with Nehat Mustafa, the Deputy Minister of Education, Science, and Technology, was surprisingly informative. He was receptive to our questions and concerns, and he gave us detailed answers as well as a book promoting developmental reforms planned for the education system, including early childhood development and preparation for university. These reforms aim towards a goal of a more modern, independent, internationally creditable institution. For example, older generations did not have to learn any English in school, and are reluctant to learn or speak in English now. My host had to learn English beginning in grade 5, similar to how we learn French beginning in Grade 4, but today, children begin to learn English by grade 3. We were allowed to join in on one of the English classes that my host attends outside of regular school hours. At first it was just a room full of high school students of varying ages who were reluctant to speak, but once they learned that our grasp of Albanian was significantly, atrociously worse than their English abilities, they openly chatted with us and told us of all their favourite places in Gjilan and in Kosovo. I couldn't help but notice that schools are ethnically separated. This is unfortunate, as isolating Serbians and Albanians from one another by separating them socially and linguistically from a very young age only further reinforces the concept of 'the other' that was so prevalent during the war. The college where we attended class, I learned, was a private Albanian university. The private universities had a reputation for not being challenging enough, while public universities were often underfunded. It seems as if some of the older students I met had ambitious goals despite their sub-par education, but luckily the quality of education has been improving, as I can see with younger students. Hopefully they soon will be able to bring both public and private schools to equal, world-wide standards.

An important part of our political education in Kosovo involved meeting with various politicians. The Speaker of the House, Jakup Krasniqi, met with us in between sessions, and Qemajl Mustafa, the mayor of Gjilan, met with us in his office. Both meetings were mainly ceremonial, beginning with a lengthy welcome and ending with a photo session, with little time to answer questions in between. While the deputy ministers we met with more readily answered our queries, these men focused the conversation more on what they wanted us to know, rather than what we were curious about. We later attended a dinner at the residence of Behgjet Pacolli, the former President of Kosovo, and the current First Deputy Prime Minister. This meeting was more interesting to many of us, as we had more time in a much more relaxed atmosphere. Also, our spare time, we met with members of the opposition movement, who had radical points of view in contrast to those we formally met with. Some of these opposition members verge on being anti-independence, preferring instead to become a province of Albania. This kind of ethnic loyalty has been a major difficulty over the course of negotiations since the war. Stefan Wolff notes that a major hindrance has been the "intransigence of local leaders to settle for nothing less than their maximum demands" in negotiations (2010). He explains that the three most important factors to successfully rebuilding after an ethnic war, and to ending tensions between the two groups, are leadership, diplomacy, and institutional design. Since Kosovo declared independence in 2008, Wolff noted that an international presence and the local leader's willingness to attend peace talks have shown promise for success in the region. However, peace has been stalled by a lack of imagination when it comes to designing institutions that could have addressed the concerns of both Serbians and Albanians. Most of the young citizens I spoke with, those in their twenties and thirties, are dissatisfied with the current political climate in Kosovo. They are unhappy with the stagnation of economic growth, the failure to achieve a peaceful independence recognized by Serbia, and they are especially upset with the ways in which post-conflict resolution had been handled by local politicians for the past fourteen years.

Kosovo aspires to become a full member of the European Union. However, there remain many challenges still to overcome on the path of transition. For example, a gender gap persists. The education system is in undergoing improvement, but post-secondary has not reached world-wide standards yet. Unemployment is rampant, with nearly half the population spending their days in cafes or begging. Political and social upheaval still exists in Mitrovica, the northern area of Kosovo which border Serbia. We were not even able to visit that area of the country, as violent tensions are ongoing. There is also the question of what to do with such a young population. In class we spoke of age pyramids, and how the pyramid will slowly flip itself as the average age of the population grows over. Canada, for example, is currently an inverted pyramid, with the majority of the nations' population at the top, edging towards retirement, and the youngest percentage in the smallest age section. This is disadvantageous because the small group at the bottom has to support the large group at the top. Kosovo, however, is the exact opposite, with a large young population creating a strong base for the older population. This is the ideal window of opportunity, in which this large base can be utilized to build the economy and the infrastructure to support their generation as they age and set up a prosperous future for the nation. At this moment in time, 100 nations have recognized Kosovo's independence, but that leaves many left to ally with Serbia in denying the county's independence. Russia, as a Member of the United Nations and the UN Security council continues to veto discussions regarding independence for Kosovo, much like they have currently been blocking UN involvement in Syria. It is difficult for Kosovo to display a national identity with conviction if it is still struggling to convince the world to recognize it as a nation to begin with. Kosovo must change the rest of the world's stereotypical perception of what the country is like. Macedonia is a good example, as they are in the process of this change at the moment. Skopje, the capital, is being reconstructed to create a historical tourist site that outwardly projects a positive

Macedonian identity. It artfully blends history and modernity, and it is beautiful and clean. I realized that for my first few days in Kosovo, like most people who had never been there, I was projecting my predetermined convictions of what I thought Kosovo would be, rather than accepting it for what it was. When I told friends and family at home where I was going, they were instantly worried. I was told it would be unclean, unfriendly, unsafe, yet I absolutely felt safe and welcome at my temporary home in Kosovo. Changing the global population's misconstrued ideas of the country is a huge hurdle Kosovo must overcome in the near future, absolutely necessary to their hopes of being recognized by all nations, catching up with modernization, and joining global development.

The Kosovo war grew out of years of tension between Serbians and Albanians in Kosovo. Both groups decided that they needed the region to brand their own national identity, and they created their identity out of opposition to one another. However, now years since Albanians won control of Kosovo and declared independence, they continue struggling to articulate a comprehensive identity that encompasses nation as a whole. I was lucky to experience the new, young nation and to watch it grow. Though the nation may still have issues transitioning from a traditional society to a modern society, they are focusing on improving their education system, their economy, and their global image. Kosovo today is in the process of forming a new, modern identity to represent this new era of Kosovar history, one that will hopefully continue to foster peaceful relations.

References

Buckley, M. & Cummings, S. 2001, *Kosovo: Perceptions of War and Its Aftermath*, BookEns LTD, London.

Fischer, B. & Schwandner-Sievers, S. 2002, *Albanian Identities: Myth and History*, Indiana University Press, Indiana.

GlobalEdge 213, Michigan State University, Michigan viewed July 20 2013, <http://globaledge.msu.edu/countries/kosovo/statistics>.

Judah, T. 2008, *Kosovo: What Everyone Needs to Know,* Oxford University Press, Oxford.

MEST 2012, *Clear Vision of Educational System Reformation,* Ministry of Education, Science, and Technology, Pristina.

Moore, C. 2001, *Contemporary Violence: Postmodern War in Kosovo and Chechnya,* Manchester University Press, Manchester.

Popolo, D. 2011, A New Science of International Relations: Modernity, Complexity and the Kosovo conflict, Ashgate Publishing LTD, Surrey.

Recognition Information and Statistics 2013, Kosovo, Viewed August 28 2013, http://www.kosovothanksyou.com/statistics/

Voorhoeve, J. 2007, *From War to Rule of Law: Peace Building after Violent Conflicts,* Amsterdam University press, Amsterdam.

Wolff, S. 2010, *The Path to Ending Ethnic Conflicts,* Video, TEDTalks, USA.

Life in a Post-Conflict Society

Anneka Sutton

FOURTEEN years ago NATO forces intervened in the autonomous province of Kosovo, after a series of "ethnic cleansing" policies had been conducted by Serbia on Albanian minorities. Serbian forces, along side Yugoslavia, had used extremely forceful measures to displace hundreds of thousands of Albanians from their Kosovo homes. NATO stepped in with their methods of humanitarian intervention demanding that all parties involved in the conflict, formed and maintained a ceasefire. This paper will discuss the war that broke out between Serbia and Kosovo in 1998, covering not only why it happened but what specifically pushed the United Nations to express grave concern for the situation and deploy NATO to help with humanitarian aid. It will then move on to discuss the current state of Kosovo and its citizens, as experienced through my own eyes as I embarked on the Balkans Peace Program 2013, over a decade since the war took place.

To begin, the conflict between Serbia and Kosovo began years earlier when Serbia not only illegally but violently annexed Kosovo's territory. The Serbian military labelled Albanians as an anti-revolution movement that posed a threat to Yugoslavia's socialist revolution, which posed them as a potential enemy to Yugoslavians and their new country. This lead Yugoslavia to use the "harshest of means, both political and military" to suppress the so-called Albanian movement (Pllana, 2010, p. 57, 58, 86, 294). The Serb Secret Service (SSS) had planned out this entire operation in order to build fear and loathing inside the minds of Yugoslavians. The creation of the impression that ethnic Albanians were a potential threat lead Yugoslavia to believe that they needed to be kept under "strict, permanent supervision, especially the new generations of intellectuals" (Pllana, 2010, p. 57, 58, 86, 294). Over many years during the mid 1900's the SSS kept this situation the same, committing harsh crimes against ethnic Albanians, treating them in extremely inhumane ways and imprisoning them. When this proved to be insufficient the SSS upped their ante and imposed threats of the existence of large weaponry in the hands of the Albanians. This claim lead to the use of the "most terrorizing punishments against an entire nation" (Pllana, 2010, p. 57, 58, 86, 294). It wasn't until years later that the international community decided to step in and force the leaders of the SSS to step down, with the notion that they should be ashamed of what they had done. The forceful removal of their leaders seemed to keep things calm until a few years later when constitutional amendments lead to Kosovo becoming a key component of Yugoslavia. This built resentment with the Serbs as they hoped to maintain control over Kosovo. As oppression began to rebuild in Kosovo, Albanians began to believe that armed resistance was the only answer to the situation at hand. Even though Kosovo had been declared an Independent 'Republic of Kosova' earlier in the year of 1991, Kosovo's independence was not yet a reality. As Tim Judah states in his book *Kosovo: War and Revenge* the independence only existed in certain forms, but "definitely not in the sense of Kosovo Albanians running Kosovo" (Judah, 2000, p. 65). Serbian institutions still remained inside Kosovo borders, and Serbian police were still very much in control. The Serb's 'ethnic cleansing' was still taking place even with the newly found independence of Kosovo, and therefore Albanians were still being penalized. In 1991 the Kosovo Liberation Army, KLA, was formed with plans to attack the Serbian law enforcement that resided in Kosovo. In February 1998, as KLA attacks intensified, the Serbs initiated an undeclared war against Kosovo, which lead to the destroying of over 500 Albanian villages, displacing hundreds of thousands of Albanian citizens from their homes. Over "1,500 Albanians, children, women, elderly, along with other civilians, all unarmed were executed barbarously while trying to escape from their villages" (Pllana, 2010, p. 57, 58, 86,

294). It was due to these atrocious acts of violence against the Albanians that the international community stepped in to help provide humanitarian aid and peace between Serbians and Albanians.

When NATO intervened between the Serbs and Albanians, it was the first time in its history that NATO went into war. Slobodan Milosevic, a Serbian, was the leader of Yugoslavia at the time and NATO was holding him responsible for the thousands of people killed and hundreds of thousands that had been displaced from their homes. In his book *Winning Ugly: NATO'S War to Save Kosovo* Michael O'Hanlon describes how the war between Serbia and Kosovo was not only affecting their own territories, but how the displacement of such a large number of people was creating humanitarian issues in the surrounding border countries of Macedonia and Albania, and yielding "consequences for stability and security across the entire region" (Daalder and O'hanlon, 2000, p. 1, 2, 4, 5). NATO's initial attempts to negotiate with Milosevic reached no benefits due to Milosevic's display of little interest in coming to any form of an agreement. This pushed NATO to begin a brief bombing campaign, the purpose of which was to "to force Milosevic back to the negotiating table so that NATO could find a way short of independence to protect Kosovo's ethnic Albanian population from Serb violence and political domination" (Daalder and O'Hanlon, 2000, p. 1, 2, 4, 5). There was never any intention by

NATO to initiate a war through these minor bombings, their only purpose was as stated, to push for further negotiations between Serbia and Albania and form a ceasefire. When the United Nations Security Council signed off on the deployment of NATO they did not expect nor prepare themselves, or the United States for a war. Bill Clinton was the President of the United States at this time, and he had "failed to prepare the country for the possibility that NATO's initial bombing raids might be the opening salvo of a drawn-out war" (Daalder and O'Hanlon, 2000, p. 1, 2, 4, 5). After quick preparations the NATO-led international force moved onto the scene, and was followed by a large amount of destruction between Albanians and Serbs as well as NATO and Serbian military. As the war persisted, Serbia continued to fight not only their Albanian opponents but many of the world's best air forces as well. Even with their great efforts, NATO was unsuccessful at first as the Serbian military dominated the earlier phases of the war while the Albanians paid the highest costs. Thousands of civilians, including children, were killed, abused, raped and expelled from their homes, while the number of Serbs who were injured or killed was incomparable to such high numbers. It wasn't until Russian President Boris Yeltsin mended previously broken ties with the United States, and committed to do whatever he could to end the war, that hope was in sight. Yeltsin initiated a negotiation process that "put a 360-degree diplomatic squeeze on

Milosevic" (Daalder and O'Hanlon, 2000, p. 1, 2, 4, 5). The international community forces began to see the Serbian forces becoming weaker as they were losing equipment and fire power due to the precision bombings that were being implemented upon them. In order for a victory to be won, NATO's attack would have to consist of more than precise bombings, and now with the help provided by Russia they had the proper assets. On the political front there was now "NATO's demonstrated cohesion as an alliance and Russia's growing willingness to cooperate in pursuit of a diplomatic solution" in addition to what was occurring on the military front; "NATO's talk of a possible ground war and the well publicized decisions to augment allied troop strength in Macedonia" (Daalder and O'Hanlon, 2000, p. 1, 2, 4, 5). Together this meant that NATO had power on both the military and political sides of the war and convinced Milosevic that no possible escape remained for him in terms of winning the war. Once this became known to Milosevic, he had only one option in order to make sure no further harm was done to Serbia or it's forces and to maintain his title within the government. In 1999 Milosevic agreed to an international peace program to end the violence, which further lead to the removal of his troops and the entrance of KFOR, the NATO-led peacekeeping force of Kosovo, into Kosovo. KFOR consisted of forces from all over Britain and North America in order to promote peace in the recently demolished and traumatized areas of Kosovo. Albanian citizens were overjoyed with the presence of KFOR within their borders and paraded the streets with flowers and gifts as KFOR members were patrolling. Even though KFOR was only positioned to implement humanitarian aid their numbers and potential power were enough to scare. As long as the forces were in Kosovo it reminded Milosevic of the military power that could be used against him if he chose to go against his agreement and wage another war. With the war over, and Kosovo citizens protected by KFOR, the question now focused on how to remove the forces from Kosovo and not have their economy and framework collapse at the same time.

Creating a desirable home for the citizens of Kosovo was not an easily attainable task. With the country filled with military forces the social situation at the time was described as "neither war, nor peace" (Pllana, 2010, p. 57, 58, 86, 294). The ongoing presence of the military and police was causing unrest throughout the population, making any sense of peace hard to find. It was time for the international community to slowly move out of Kosovo, in order to let it's citizens return to their lives and begin rebuilding their economy themselves. Overtime KFOR began to hand over duties to the Kosovo police to remove responsibility from their hands and to gradually make their presence unnecessary. The hope was to rebuild Kosovo from the inside out, and prepare it's structures to be able to stand on their own. The international community maintained a large portion of control over Kosovo at this time due to their help in ending the war and providing aid. External pressures on Kosovo's government were great as the international community hoped to help Kosovo move forward in the same ways that their own countries had before. One of the main pressures was to incorporate more women in the political sphere. Gender quota laws were enacted requiring a significant portion of candidates to be women. The international community, while still worried about remaining tensions between Albanians and Serbians, also hoped to create a safe and happy environment in Kosovo for both ethnicities. Ethnic diversity was thus an important component of the newly formed Kosovo as it would help to minimize the tensions that initially caused the war. While it would be extremely difficult to forgive and move past the horrific events of the war with Serbia, some form of reconciliation needed to be found between the two conflicting ethnicities in order to move forward.

During the war hundreds of thousands of albanians were displaced from Kosovo, being forced to evacuate their homes and move across the continent or even the globe. Once the war was over, the government of Kosovo alongside the international community made it their mission to bring these refugees back home. One of their greatest challenges was not the actual act of bringing these people back, but rather creating a home that they would want to come back to. After the war Kosovo was left with a severely crippled economy. Housing and land was hard to find in the area and the unemployment rate was sky rocketing. This left little reason for displaced refugees to want to return to their home land. While they may still have family back in Kosovo, the majority of people had begun new lives with jobs and houses in countries all over the world. There would be no purpose in returning to a country where they would most likely not have a job and even if they could find one it would be poorly paid. In addition to housing and job insecurities Kosovo was also crippled with a low availability of public services as well as limitations on freedom of movement around the continent and world. Healthcare and unemployment or disability funding are very uncommon and therefore difficult to find. The few jobs that are available rarely come with insurance for the employee or their family. With new lives that include greater benefits and security for refugees and their families, Kosovo would have to offer allot more then heritage to draw people back into it's borders.

I'd like to take a moment here to share a brief part of my trip to Kosovo this summer, over a decade after the war ended. It is needless to say that when I took off from Toronto airport in May 2013 I could never prepare myself for the culture shock that I was about to experience. While I had always known that I was blessed with a life full of opportunities it truly became clear to me once I embarked on the Balkans Peace Program 2013. Over the past few years I have been lucky to travel all over the world too poverty stricken areas in order to help provide missionary assistance, and yet none of these experiences could compare. While Kosovo was not suffering from the extreme cases of poverty I had seen previously the people there were secluded from many opportunities that others such as myself take for granted. To begin, as stated earlier Kosovo's unemployment rate is over fifty percent when students are calculated into the equation. Here in Canada when our unemployment rate wavers on ten percent we feel panicked and in need of an economic 'fix'. Our daily activities highlighted this extreme unemployment as multiple times a day we would go to one of the many coffee shops that would be packed full of people. Due to the fact that many adults do not have jobs, they instead resort to spending almost every hour of their day walking from one coffee shop to the next. The other participants and I also found the prices to be quite low, which is a result of customers not having a high income if one at all. For the people that did have jobs, be it part time or full time, wages were extremely inferior to those here in Canada. The current minimum wage in Canada is $10.25, while in Kosovo many of the men and women who accompanied us on our trip had part time jobs where they were receiving three to four euros an hour. While the currency is different, this amount would still only convert to about four to five dollars per hour, which is less then half of what students earn back in Canada. After learning this I could not imagine getting paid anywhere near this amount, even if retailer prices were lower. If I were to imagine myself as a person who had been displaced during the Kosovo war, the same thoughts would be crossing my mind. I would have a life in a new country where I could be given employment and receive enough money to support myself and my family so why would I chose to have all of this taken away from me? The next issue I would like to address is that of health care. During my three weeks in Kosovo the group and I came across multiple sidewalk stands where people were asking for money for children in need. Children with diseases and physical disabilities that required specific and urgent life saving surgery. Two problems arise for families in these situations, the first being that they do not have the money to pay for the medical bills and surgery that their child requires. The second problem is that even if they did have the funding, there are no doctors in Kosovo that are able to perform these life saving surgeries that the children need. The former issue derives from the lack of employment discussed earlier. Families who receive an income typically rely on a single member of the household, commonly the father, to support themselves. A single income is then required to pay for housing, food, clothes, schooling and health care, as well as any unlisted extras. Being in this situation makes it hard enough to support a standard family of four, let alone to support a family that struggles with a disabled or diseased child. The latter issue focuses on the lack of local educated doctors who are capable of performing life saving surgeries. When I asked about the educational system that doctors in Kosovo had to attend in order to receive their medical licenses, many locals responded to me by saying that their local doctors were only able to do minor treatments, and in cases where patients required more serious care, such as major surgery, they had to leave the country in order to find a doctor who could help them. Most locals discussed how whenever someone in their families required serious help they went to Switzerland in order to find it. My host family's grandmother had to undergo a triple bypass surgery in the past and in order for her to receive the medical care she required, her and her husband had to travel to Switzerland where they stayed for a couple months until she was well enough to come back home to Kosovo. As my trip continued we witnessed first hand the desperateness of a local young boys family who were exhausting all their outlets in order to raise money to help treat his illnesses. After seeing dozens of posters placed all over town as well as people marching through the streets begging for money to help this boy, our group decided to attend a fundraiser that was being held for him at a local club. The atmosphere that night was unexplainable as hundreds of people gathered to help this family. It wasn't until the end of the night that a gentleman stepped forward and gave this family the greatest gift they could ask for. An older gentleman who lives in Switzerland walked up to the microphone and told the family that he would personally adopt this child as his own and take him back to Switzerland with himself where he would be able to get the medical care that the child required. It was a moment like no other as everyone cheered and screamed in excitement and joy, yet at the same time I could not help but think about how if this situation had taken place back in Canada it would be completely different. In general Canadians, myself included, take our healthcare system for granted. While having a severely handicapped child is always some degree of a burden on a family, be it financially or emotionally, this burden can not be compared to similar situations in developing nations such as Kosovo where families have little hope in financial support. Canada's universal healthcare provides families with a sense of hope as it finances life saving surgery as well as therapy for people in need. Canadians are not burdened by the extensive funds that are required to help give their family members an opportunity for a useful life, while Kosovars do have to carry this burden and find their own ways to raise money locally. I personally believe that it is wrong for a family who is already suffering from the stress of having a disabled child, to then have to worry about how to pay for this child's well being. In 2011 the Government of Kosovo stated that one of their main objectives was "Increasing the quality of health services in a way that public and private health institutions may provide services that are as close as possible to international standards and therefore reducing the need for treatment abroad" (Hodgetts, 2012, p. 3, 7). They plan to implement a new law on health throughout the country that will provide better health services and healthcare for Kosovo's citizens, however the implementation of this law could take up to three years or more. One of the main reasons for this delay is the method in which the government is planning to finance this new health system. They are currently planning to put 5% of gross wages from employers towards Health insurance. Unfortunately however, this has caused debate as there are too few registered tax paying employees to fund a successful and sustainable insurance fund. Therefore structural reforms are going to have to take place before a sustainable health insurance system can be implemented, which is going to take time.

While the lack of health insurance is a main cause for debate in Kosovo, so is the subject of low wages for medical staff. In Canada individuals who work in the medical field, doctors, nurses etc., are amongst the highest paid careers in the country. This is not the case in Kosovo where a Specialist Doctor has a monthly income of less then four hundred dollars a month (Hodgetts, 2012, p. 3, 7). Aggravation spreads through the medical fields due to these statistics, firing many debates and protests. In 2009 over fifteen hundred health care workers marched through the streets of Prishtina demanding higher salaries, many of whom carried signs that read "Do not forget us, help us, we save lives." (Hodgetts, 2012, p. 3, 7). Doctors in Kosovo are humiliated in the international community when other physicians around the world find out how much they make a year. Many of them even have had to make their family a social assistance case as they can not adequately support their family on their yearly incomes. Low wages indirectly affect many other sections of the health care system other than Doctors annual income. For instance Doctors have to undergo years of educational training in order to get their positions. When students discover that the medical field does not pay well and will not help them support their families they become discouraged and many choose to pick a different career path. This does not help the citizens of Kosovo who are already struggling with a small number of local doctors to help provide care. Aggravated medical staff can also have a negative impact on the quality of the health care that they provide. All of these situations are simply further leading to a poor health care structure for the people of Kosovo.

High unemployment and a failed health care system has pressured Kosovo citizens to feel the need to emigrate to countries where they would be able to live more sustainable lives. Almost each of the Albanian hosts, who were housing myself and the other members of the Balkans Peace Program 2013, shared their feeling towards this subject. They asked countless questions as to how our lives were back at home in Canada and what differences we noticed between our lives and theirs. They would then continue to share their dreams of moving out of Kosovo, most wanting to live in Canada, and getting jobs in career fields such as teaching and veterinary schooling. Unfortunately these dreams would not be very easy to accomplish. Due to the high number of Kosovo citizens who have emigrated in the past decade, Kosovo citizens are required to be issued a travel visa from each country they plan to visit. Apart from Albania, Macedonia, Montenegro and the Maldives Islands Kosovo's citizens need to file for a visa that will state their reason for travel and the length of their visit. If they are carrying a passport from the Republic of Kosovo citizens are able to travel in and out of Turkey as well. These visas allow the government of Kosovo to control the leaving of their citizens to other countries. In order for a visa to be issued, citizens are required to fill out paperwork, have a Republic of Kosovo passport in their possession, and get their application approved by the ministry of foreign affairs in the country of their choosing. Our hosts explained to us how extremely difficult it was for Kosovo citizens to attain any form of travel visa, many of them had tried before and had been denied. On top of the paper work and time it takes to file for a visa it also costs a great amount of money each time an individual submits an application. The only place that a few of the hosts had attained visas for in the past was Switzerland and they were generally issued in order to visit family who had emigrated during the war or for medical purposes as discussed earlier. As a citizen of Canada, I take it for granted how easy it is for me to travel around the world. Canadians are rarely required to apply for visas in order to travel internationally, and are welcomed in to other country's borders for the purpose of travel, work, school, or even relocation without much hassle. I have had the opportunity to travel all over North and South America as well as Europe in my lifetime, and I could not even begin to imagine what my life would be like had I not been given such opportunities. Kosovo is almost one thousandth the size of Canada, with an area of 10,908 km, taking only a few hours to drive from one side to the other. Canada on the other hand takes multiple days of driving to cross, possessing miles of land to discover and explore. Even if leaving the borders of Canada was difficult there would still be hundreds of places to travel to, and multiple opportunities available nation wide for housing and work. It is therefore no surprise that the greater population of Kosovo, especially the younger generations, hope to leave and find a life elsewhere. The tighter that the restraints are on emigrating out of the country, the greater the want to leave is becoming. In order for the government of Kosovo to effectively lower the rates of emigration, they need to first create an economy that their citizens will want to grow up in, be educated in and eventually begin a family in.

One aspect of Kosovo life that was very clearly displayed by it's citizens was the importance of family. Within my first two days of living at my host family's house I had already been introduced to the majority of her family. Cousins, Grandparents, Uncles and Aunts from both her mothers and her father's side of the family were constantly visiting the house for lunch and dinner, an occurrence that does not happen often with Canadian families. While this could very easily be due to the fact that family members are not easily able to move very far from each other due to the requirement of visas, it was very clear that Kosovo citizens are extremely family oriented, which is an aspect of life that I would love to see more of in Canada and throughout many other countries around the world. It is not very common in Canada that family members see each other more than a few times a year, and when they do see one another it is typically for specific purposes such as holidays and birthdays. Most children move out of their parents house and into either residence or their own apartments after high school in order to start their own adult lives, or to begin their post secondary schooling. This results in family members being spread throughout the country or even throughout the world, making it very difficult to stop by for dinner every night. In Kosovo however, family members tend to live extremely close to one another, and visit each other often. Grandparents are extremely involved in their grandchildren's lives, and in some cases even live in the same house as the children grow up. I believe that this strong importance on family that Kosovo citizens have plays an important role in bringing happiness and peace of mind into their everyday culture and life.

Before my university professor emailed me the link to the Balkans Peace Program 2013 I knew nothing about the war between Kosovo and Serbia that took place over a decade ago. I will admit that I did not even know Kosovo was a country, and it was not until I did further research into the program that I became aware of the struggles and severe hardships that Kosovo Albanians had undergone. This trip has really opened my eyes to the conflicts that are occurring all around the world and how they are not receiving the media attention that they deserve. The Balkans Peace Program gave students like myself a chance to be immersed directly into the Albanian life fourteen years after the war had taken place. We were able to see how students around our own ages lived in a post war society, and hear from the locals how the war affected them, at the time and currently, and what the government was doing to help. At the same time we did get to have in depth meetings with members of the Kosovo government to hear how they have arranged budgets and created programs in order to help rebuild their country's economy. While these meetings were very informative and provided us with a great deal of information on how the government is planning to help it's citizens, to me there is nothing better then hearing and learning straight from the locals. Although the government officials were extremely polite and enlightening, there were multiple instances where the information that was disclosed to us contested the information that the locals were presenting. An example of this would be when we were discussing Kosovo's education plans, and asked about the willingness to accept Serbian children in Albanian schools. We were told during our meeting that they were working on fixing the tensions between Serbian and Albanian Kosovo citizens. However this was not the case when we visited high schools across the country. They were segregated, Serbian schools for the Serbian Kosovo citizens, and Albanian schools for Albanian Kosovo citizens. The information that we were receiving was constantly being contested by our hosts once we were out of the government offices, and the concern for their people that was being voiced to us by government officials felt discredited as they drove away in brand new extremely expensive vehicles.

As a Political Science student I have studied multiple different conflicts from all over the globe, yet Wikipedia and scholarly books or journals can never compete with the ability to directly talk to the local people who experienced the real thing. This form of hands on learning is incomparable to anything that a professor could have taught us in a classroom with a video projector, and is an opportunity that I am exceptionally thrilled to have been given. The separation controversy of the former

Yugoslavia has come to an end and Kosovo has become recognized on the international level as an independent country. A sense of peace from the previous years of war and turmoil now fill the population of Kosovo. As this country begins to redevelop its economy in a post conflict state, it faces many challenges along its path and has many obstacles that need to be overcome. This paper has discussed the war between Kosovo and Serbia, starting with the origins and moving on to the outbreak and duration of the war itself. It has discussed the conflicts that Kosovo has faced in the past and is facing currently. While change is slow, the citizens of Kosovo have high hopes for their newly independent country and although it seems there is allot that needs to be done to better their economy progress, while slow is steadily developing.

References

Daalder, I. and O'hanlon, M. 2000. *Winning ugly*. Washington, D.C.: Brookings Institution Press, p. 1, 2, 4, 5.

Hodgetts, A. 2012. Investigation Into Public Health Care In Kosovo. *Balkan Policy Institute*, p. 3, 7. [Accessed: 31 Aug 2013].

Judah, T. 2000. *Kosovo*. New Haven: Yale University Press, p. 65.

Pllana, N. 2010. *Intervenimi i NATO-s në Kosovë*. Prishtinë: Botues Radio Kosova e Lirë, p. 57, 58, 86, 294.

The Evolution of the Kosovo Security Force

Roderick Kelly

Introduction and Background

> "Currently, half the countries emerging from violent conflict revert to
> conflict within five years".[23]
> Kofi Annan, In Larger Freedom, UN Doc. 59/2005

On 24 March 1999, the North Atlantic Treaty
Organization (NATO) deliberately intervened in Kosovo in
attempt to avert a humanitarian crisis. When Operation
ALLIED FORCE began, NATO did not have a United Nations
(UN) mandate yet despite this, they began dropping bombings
targeting Serbian forces.[24] The air campaign halted the
humanitarian catastrophe that was then unfolding in Kosovo.[25]
The decision to intervene followed more than a year of fighting
within Kosovo and the failure of international efforts to resolve
the conflict by diplomatic means.[26] This intervention action
arguably saved hundreds if not thousands of Kosovar citizens'

---

[23] (Voorhoeve, 2007) Kofi Annan, In Larger Freedom, UN Doc. 59/2005.
[24] (The Kosovo Air Campaign, 2012)
[25] (The Kosovo Air Campaign, 2012)
[26] (The Kosovo Air Campaign, 2012)

lives. Following the air campaign, the United Nations Security Council Resolution (UNSCR) 1244 placed Kosovo under the authority of the United Nations Interim Administration Mission in Kosovo (UNMIK), through which security would be provided by the NATO-led Kosovo Force (KFOR).[27]

In most cases following conflict there is a risky period of lawlessness and post-war looting. It is during this period that military rule (either via the UN, NATO or otherwise), interim government, and transitional justice must be enacted.[28] The international community must respond quickly to implement a transitional government and security force to restore rule of law in efforts to restore security and prevent a bad situation from becoming much worst.[29]

---

[27] (United Nations Interim Administration in Kosovo (UNMIK), 2013) UN Resolution 1244 was approved on 10 June 1999; it authorized the Secretary-General to establish an international civil presence in Kosovo. The mission was called the United Nations Interim Administration Mission in Kosovo (UNMIK). This mission was to provide an interim administration for which the people of Kosovo could enjoy substantial autonomy. This task was unprecedented in complexity and scope; the Council vested UNMIK with authority over the territory and people of Kosovo, including all legislative and executive powers and administration of the judiciary.

[28] (Voorhoeve, 2007) p. 11.

[29] Despite operational strains of maintaining a prolonged air bombing campaign, the Alliance of NATO partners held together during 78 days of air strikes. During the period from 24 March to 10 June 1999, in which more than 38,000 sorties (individual aircraft missions) were flown and 10,484 of them were strike sorties, all without a single Allied fatality. This demonstration of air superiority demonstrates the cohesion and professionalism of the NATO partners involved in the air campaign.

The first task was to target the Federal Republic of Yugoslavia's air defences, following this, NATO gradually escalated the campaign using the most advanced, precision-guided munitions (PGM) systems thus avoiding

On 12 June 1999, directly following hostilities, the first KFOR elements entered Kosovo.[30] As dictated in the Military Technical Agreement of 9 June 1999, the deployment of the security force, KFOR, was to be synchronized with the departure of Serb security forces from Kosovo.[31] KFOR entered Kosovo on 12 June 1999 two days after the adoption of UNSCR 1244.[32] By 20 June, the Serb withdrawal was complete and KFOR was well established in Kosovo.[33] At its full strength KFOR was comprised of over 50,000 personnel.[34] KFOR being a multinational force was under unified Command and Control (C2) with substantial NATO participation.[35] During follow on discussions, agreement had been reached for the participation by

---

civilian casualties to the greatest extent possible. Target selection was reviewed at multiple levels of command to ensure that it complied with international law, was militarily justified, and minimized the risk to civilian lives and property. These collateral damage estimates are a key factor in the targeting cycle.

Having intervened in Kosovo to protect ethnic Albanians from ethnic cleansing, NATO has been equally committed to protecting Kosovo's ethnic Serbs from a similar fate since the deployment of KFOR in the province in June 1999.

[30] (The Kosovo Air Campaign, 2012)

[31] (ACO.NATO.INT, 1999) Military Technical Agreement, signed 9 June 1999 by KFOR and representatives of the Yugoslav Army and Interior Police. This agreement called for the immediate cessation of hostilities and sets the timelines for the withdrawal of Yugoslav forces from Kosovo. This involved the marking and clearing of mine-fields, booby traps and obstacles.

[32] (United Nations Interim Administration in Kosovo (UNMIK), 2013)

[33] (The Kosovo Air Campaign, 2012)

[34] (The Kosovo Air Campaign, 2012)

[35] (The Kosovo Air Campaign, 2012)

the Russian Federation.[36] More than twelve other non-NATO nations had also indicated their intention to contribute to KFOR.

The Kosovo Liberation Army (KLA) was an ethnic-Albanian paramilitary organization which sought the separation of Kosovo from Yugoslavia during the 1990s.[37] Its campaign against Yugoslav security forces precipitated a major Yugoslav military crackdown which eventually led to the Kosovo War.[38] The Kosovo Protection Corps (KPC) was formed from a small portion of the Kosovo Liberation Army (KLA) as part of the demobilization of the KLA.[39] During the fall of 1999, this new force, the KPC comprised of over 3,000 men and women came into fruition.[40] The rationale, at the time was based on traditional post-conflict theory where foreign trainers (in this case NATO forces) would assume full responsibility for the supervision of irregular forces such as the KLA and transition them into a regular army over a period of time and under strict supervision. This transition was not without its own challenges, taking a paramilitary organization such as the KLA and growing them into a multi-ethnic professional force such as the Kosovo Security Force (KSF) of today was a demanding and complex process. It should be noted that under UN Resolution 1244 there was no agreement for this type of activity, thus further

---

[36] (The Kosovo Air Campaign, 2012)

[37] (Pond, 2006)

[38] (Pond, 2006)

[39] (Pettifer, 2003)

[40] (Pettifer, 2003)

agreements has to be resolved to allow for the demilitarization and transformation of the KLA.[41] After Kosovo declared independence, the next step was to develop a professional security force, a force that will continue to evolve and become the professional Kosovo Army of the future. The KSF have created the foundation through military doctrine, training and structure to become the future Kosovo Army comprised of multi-ethnic professional men and women devoted to serving Kosovo.

The KSF - The Beginning

When the KSF was stood up on 21 January 2009, as the first Commander of the KSF, Lieutenant-General Sylejman Selimi planned to implement as his initial priority a draft military doctrine with emphasis on command and control and the core functions, this would become the Kosovo Security Strategy.[42]

---

[41] (ACO.NATO.INT, 1999) The Russian Federation agrees to participate in KFOR. This commitment is referred to as the "Helsinki Agreement".

[42] (Force, 2010) Sylejman Selimi was the first Commander of the Security Force of the Republic of Kosovo. He left this position in 2011 and became the ambassador to Albania. Selimi was born on 25 September, 1970 in Açarevë village Drenica. He finished primary education in his home town, attended his high school in Kline and finished his studies at the Faculty of Mining and Metallurgy in Kosovska Mitrovica.

With the approval of the Constitution of Kosovo, the drafting and approval process of a certain number of laws which had been foreseen with the Comprehensive Proposal for the Kosovo Status Settlement begins. One of these laws was the Law on the establishment of the Kosovo Security Council approved in the Assembly in March 2008, which was mandated to also develop the Kosovo Security Strategy. A key document and vital piece of

The Kosovo Security Council which was approved in the Assembly in March 2008 was mandated to develop the Kosovo Security Strategy.[43] This strategy would lay the foundation and allow the KSF to evolve into a professional military force. Military doctrine provides a common frame of reference across the military as a whole and helps standardize operations, facilitating readiness by establishing common ways of accomplishing military tasks. In order to complete the transition from an initial capabilities force the KSF would have to become a self-sustaining military force capable of recruiting, training and force generating professional soldiers equipped and ready for operations as dictated by their mandate.

Kosovo's Independence

In order for Kosovo to own its own self-sustaining legitimate military resources; it would first have to become a sovereign nation, so on 17 February 2008, Kosovo declared independence.[44] As a sovereign nation, a country must have foreign diplomatic relations with other nations. As a step in the right direction, on 19 March 2008, United States (US) President George W. Bush authorized military aid to the KSF in an effort

---

the Kosovo Military Doctrine that was drafted under Lt-General Selimi's command of the KSF.
[43] (Rushiti, 2013) p 5.
[44] (Associated Free Press, 2008)

to establish formal diplomatic relations with Kosovo.[45] On 4 January 2009, the names of those who were to be selected for the KSF from the ranks of the KPC were announced. After the list of names had been vetted by NATO, roughly 1,400 former members of the KPC were selected to serve as officers and enlisted ranks of the initial KSF.[46]

On 21 January 2009, the Kosovo Security Force was officially launched.[47] The KSF initially did not replace the KPC, until the KPC was disbanded several months later. KFOR was charged with mentoring the KSF and bringing the force to Full Operational Capability (FOC).[48] As part of this effort, KFOR have provided assistance to the force on a bilateral basis including logistical support such as uniforms which were supplied by the United States and vehicles which were donated by Germany.[49] Mentoring efforts were enacted and were meant to develop the KSF in line with NATO standards.[50] Additionally, Italy, Portugal and other NATO members helped the KSF by donations and training assistance.[51]

On 15 September 2009, the KSF officially began the work, with its initial operational capacities (IOC) following eight

---

[45] (Associated Free Press, 2008)
[46] (Force, 2010)
[47] (Ministry for the Kosovo Security Forces)
[48] (Force, 2010)
[49] (Force, 2010)
[50] (Force, 2010)
[51] (Force, 2010)

months of training with NATO instructors.[52] One of the first international deployments of KSF occurred in 2010, when the KSF deployed to northern Albania on two separate occasions to perform flood relief operations in support of the Albanian domestic response.[53] It is these types of contingency operations that build a military's historical character eventually allowing for autonomy.

The KSF Mission

The mission of the KSF is to conduct crisis response operations in Kosovo and abroad; civil protection operations within Kosovo; and to assist the civil authorities in responding to natural disasters and other emergencies.[54] These types of domestic mission functions form the basis of military doctrine.[55] As the KSF is a newly formed security force it is logical that these types of domestic contingency missions be captured doctrinally as priority. The KSF today is a professional, multi-ethnic, lightly armed and uniformed security force; they are subject to democratic, civilian control as with any other

---

[52] (Force, 2010)

[53] (Force, 2010)

[54] (Ministry for the Kosovo Security Forces)

[55] Reserve Forces compliment Regular Forces in times of war. In peacetime, reservists can be utilized in internal security duties and disaster relief, sparing reliance on the regular military forces, and in many countries where military roles outside of warfare are restricted, reservists are specifically exempted from these restrictions.

sovereign democratic nation.[56]   The KSF is the primary national level asset tasked with protecting its civilians. Such duties will include search and rescue operations; explosive ordnance disposal (de-mining and UXO [Unexploded Explosive Ordnance] removal). Other functions include the control and clearance of hazardous materials (HAZMAT); fire-fighting; and other humanitarian assistance tasks as needed. The KSF as a multi-ethnic force will represent and protect all the people of Kosovo.

The Ministry for the Kosovo Security Force (MKSF) is responsible for exercising civilian control over the Kosovo Security Force (KSF), including management and administration. It comprises a mixture of civilian and KSF personnel and is accountable, through the Prime Minister, to the Kosovo Assembly. The mission of the MKSF, which is also the highest level KSF Headquarters, is to formulate, implement, evaluate and develop the policies and activities of the KSF within a framework of democratic governance and in accordance with the Constitution and laws of the Republic of Kosovo.

On 22 November 2011, Lieutenant-General Sylejman Selimi retired from the KSF and President Atifete Jahjaga appointed the former Director of Operations Major-General Kadri Kastrati to succeed him as Commander of the KSF.

---

[56] (Ministry for the Kosovo Security Forces)

President Jahjaga also appointed Kastrati to the rank of Lieutenant-General when he took command of the KSF.[57]

Professionalism and Military Structure

As important is the implementation of military doctrine, the KSF were required to incorporate a military rank and insignia system as is common practice with all military organizations. Figure 1, outlines the rank and insignia that have been adopted by the KSF. Building on the traditions and history of a military organization are the backbone of the entire military culture. Having a structured chain of command is one of the core principles of Command and Control; it is with clear representation of the unity of command that leadership provides the core foundation for a professional military organization.

---

[57] Lieutenant General Kadri Kastrati, was born on March 15, 1960 in village Velikorekë (now Katunishtë), Municipality of Podujeva. He holds a Master (MA) degree in the field of security, his main topic of studies was "Disaster Management in the Republic of Kosovo and the region."

Figure 1: KSF Rank Insignia.[58]

The basic structure of a military organization is a 'unit', a 'unit' is a specialized group of members often trained to a similar skillset and having support functions built in to allow the unit to be self-contained.[59] The KSF is comprised of multiple units, of varying skillsets giving the force a ranging military capability. Figure 2, indicates the KSF units that make up the military structure of the KSF. The Rapid Reaction Brigade would be the high readiness response unit; supporting units include elements of Communications Company, Operational Support Brigade, Logistics Battalion and Medical Company. Other specialized

---

[58] (Ministry for the Kosovo Security Forces)
[59] A typical unit is a homogeneous military organization (combat, combat-support or non-combat in capability) that includes service personnel predominantly from a single arm of service, or a branch of service, and it's administrative and command functions are self-contained.

units such as Helicopter Unit provide support functions that increase the capability and mobility of the KSF. The representation of units, brigades, company's and battalion's within the KSF indicates a strong foundation adhering to military doctrine and practices of a modern military force. Military capability is produced by combining assigned resources to accomplish a given mission.

Figure 2: KSF Unit Emblems.[60]

Declaration of Full Operational Capability (FOC)

In recent months the KSF has achieved an important historical milestone. Minister Agim Ceku was very confident in early 2013 when he announced to parliament that, "2013 was going to be the year of the Kosovo Army".[61] For comparison, in 2009, the KSF was a lightly-armed force composed of 2,500

---

[60] (Ministry for the Kosovo Security Forces)
[61] (Kabashhaj, 2013)

101

Regular and 800 Reserve members, whose primary mission was crisis response.[62]   Five years after declaring independence from Serbia, Kosovo's 2,500 member KSF had reached "full operational capability" (FOC), NATO declared on 9 July 2013.[63] NATO Secretary-General Andrs Fogh Rasmussen, said in a news release, "The Kosovo Security Force has reached full operational capability and is fully capable of performing the tasks assigned to it within its mandate, to standards designated by NATO".[64] Having now accomplished this milestone, what does the future hold for the KSF?

The Future for the KSF

What are the threats, interests and potential courses of action in structuring the future Kosovo Security Force?   Since Kosovo declared its independence in 2008 and despite some minor inter-ethnic frictions; it has since enjoyed a period of relative stability.[65]   As with many other regional countries, Kosovo still faces challenges of weak government institutions and rule of law.[66]   Arguably, potential external threats to the national security of Kosovo are international organized crime, illegal migration, international terrorism and the potential spread

---

[62] (Kabashhaj, 2013)
[63] (Vandiver, 2013)
[64] (Vandiver, 2013)
[65] (Muja, 2013)
[66] (Muja, 2013)

of weapons of mass destruction.[67]   Kosovo is challenged internally by indirect and unpredictable threats, these include; the political developments in Western Balkans, the impact of economic crisis and low levels of socio-economic development, environmental challenges and threats stemming from globalization and technological developments.[68] These threats will be reduced as the government institutions become more established and as the economy grows to become more sustainable.

The situation in Eastern Europe has changed dramatically in the last decade. Kosovo is no longer under any imminent military threat.[69] While political disputes and rivalries in Western Balkan states still persist, all national armies are going through a process of reform and downsizing.[70] Balkan states are moving their military forces towards membership with formal alliances that improve stability in the region. As an example of progress, Croatia and Albania have recently become NATO members as of 1 April 2009.[71]

---

[67] (Muja, 2013)

[68] (Muja, 2013)

[69] (Muja, 2013)

[70] (Muja, 2013)

[71] (NATO.int, 2013) The most recent accessions to NATO membership are those of Albania (Kosovo's boarding neighbor) and Croatia.   Albania had participated in the Member Accession Program (MAP) since its inception in 1999 and Croatia joined in 2002. They worked with NATO in a wide range of areas, with particular emphasis on defence and security sector reform, as well as support for wider democratic and institutional reform.

Kosovo along with countries in the region are small and lack the resources to tackle global threats, thus necessitating their participation in combined and international operations.[72] The unpredictable nature and scope of global threats require that nations aim to build multi-purpose security forces that are able to adapt and react quickly to global dynamics.[73]

For future operations the KSF would have to be combat ready to provide rapid reaction forces to any potential crisis and be prepared for quick deployment to support these operations.[74] The KSF should also be able to react to a diverse nature of threats including those related to territorial integrity, maintaining an ability to respond to international crisis and peace-building operations and provide responsiveness to any natural and emergency situations.[75] At present, the KSF is equipped and ready for these types of missions on a small scale. They have deployed to bordering Albania in support of flood relief operations. Future operating environments could be drastically different and involve a more specialized force.

Changes in the strategic environment will also dictate the type of exercises the KSF will participate, the types of partnerships they engage in, how they development national

---

In July 2008, they both signed Accession Protocols and became official members of the NATO Alliance on 1 April 2009.
[72] (Muja, 2013)
[73] (Muja, 2013)
[74] (Muja, 2013)
[75] (Muja, 2013)

concepts and security doctrine, and the procurement of various military equipment to fulfill these roles.[76]

As the international security atmosphere has evolved, unconventional asymmetric warfare are taking the place of conventional forces in modern warfare.[77] A future role for the KSF could be expansion of capabilities to include the development of Special Forces strictly for a counter-terrorism function. This would allow the KSF to participate in the 'Global War on Terror' and contribute strategically to international security.

---

[76] (Muja, 2013)   As an example of current operations, the KSF will be conducting a Field Exercise, EAGLE 2, in October 2013, which will be implemented in several regions of Kosovo (Ministry for the Kosovo Security Forces). For this purpose the KSF has made all preparations and preliminary agreements with municipalities and all institutions that will be part of this exercise in order to develop the exercise as planned.

The purpose of this exercise for the KSF is to test command skills, reaction and coordination of Units, Headquarters, members in the terrain, and overall Command and Control (C2). Convoys of the KSF will march from their bases in Pristina, Prizren, Gjilan, Mitrovica, and Pomozotin to the rendezvous (RV) points of gathering areas and activity will be concentrated in the municipalities such as; Pec, Istok, Prizren and Kline.

The Ministry for Kosovo Security Force and the KSF announced publically for situational awareness of all citizens that the movements of the convoys on highways and local roads will be observed during the first ten days of October and will be done only for exercise purposes.

These types of C2 exercises can be expected annually for any typical military, in the coming years the KSF will expand these types of exercises to become Joint or Combined operations with other nation's military forces.

[77] (Muja, 2013) Unconventional Warfare consists of activities conducted to enable a resistance movement or insurgency to coerce, disrupt or overthrow an occupying power or government by operating through or with an underground, auxiliary and guerrilla force in a denied area.

Potential epansion of the KSF Air Force assets would involve significant investment by the Kosovo government but it would be an investment into a capability that would act as a force multiplier to current KSF assets and resources. Military capability and equipment procurement expansion would carry a heavy price tag, a cost that may not be feasible for Kosovo's immediate foreseeable future. It is likely more realistic and feasible a least for the near term that the KSF focus on the current initiatives outlined in their existing doctrine given the country's economic situation.

Kosovo will continue to need security initiatives that will contain and prevent regional political tensions. Serbia continues to challenge the legality of Kosovo's declaration of independence. The Belgrade authorities have refrained from direct interference but have continued to obstruct the strengthening and expansion of authority of Kosovo institutions in general and those of security related in particular.[78] Serbia continues to finance and operate parallel administrative and security institutions in Serb-dominated areas in Kosovo, actions that continue to obstruct Kosovo's sovereignty.[79] These are but a few reasons why Kosovo must continue to expand the KSF as the country gains fully-recognized independence.

---

[78] (Muja, 2013)
[79] (Muja, 2013)

Conclusions

Kosovo's declaration of independence in February 2008 came nearly nine years after Operation *ALLIED FORCE*, NATOs bombing campaign to end Serbia's use of force against Kosovo's ethnic Albanian majority. Of the 50,000 NATO troops who moved into Kosovo in 1999 to oversee Serbia's withdrawal, only 5,000 remain today.[80] These soldiers remain onsite and continue to contribute to the peace and security of the region. The rift between the Albanian majority and ethnic Serbs (whom still refuse to recognize the government of Kosovo) still exists and will likely continue for generations.[81]

Political and ethnic tensions have significantly declined in the past year. Kosovo's leaders have their sights set on a new goal, eventual NATO membership.[82] To achieve this goal Kosovo has had to develop a small army or defense force of its own. The KSF is that force, it has evolved since the end of the war from the remnants of the KLA, to the KPC and now exists as a 'professional' multi-ethnic security force that is on the road to becoming a 'professional' military force. Last year, Minister Agim Ceku, the current minister of the KSF, and former Prime-Minister, also echoed that sentiment in his remarks, "a Military force is [a] very good instrument for modernizing society. Here

---

[80] (Vandiver, 2013)
[81] (Vandiver, 2013)
[82] (Vandiver, 2013)

we can serve as [an] example, good example, of discipline, service to a nation, commitment to duty".[83]

The KSF is a professional multi-ethnic security force that is on the path to becoming a professional military. The basic doctrine, foundations and structures are in place to provide military capability, it is now up to the government of Kosovo and the guidance of NATO to allow the KSF to evolve and grow to the next level by providing the funding, support and resources needed to reach the goal of becoming a sustainable professional army.

There still remain obstacles for Kosovo to overcome. Approximately 100 countries have recognized Kosovo's independence in the past five years.[84] Yet Kosovo remains outside the United Nations due to opposition by Serbia, Russia, China and other member states.[85] While the U.S. supports and backs Kosovo's independence, U.S. officials have not yet offered a clear endorsement of Kosovo's ambitions for a proper military force.[86] Embassy officials in Pristina have said that the U.S. supports the current model of the KSF and the ongoing security sector review that is being guided by U.S. military advisers.[87] The cautiousness of the U.S. is likely derived from previous post-conflict experience, given that over half of nations involved in

---

[83] (Vandiver, 2013)
[84] (Vandiver, 2013)
[85] (Vandiver, 2013)
[86] (Vandiver, 2013)
[87] (Vandiver, 2013)

conflict revert back to conflict within five years. The level of endorsement the U.S. and other NATO members will support for a Kosovo military force will be conscientious and risk managed for years to come, but at some point, Kosovo will become fully on its own, a sovereign nation. Kosovars are a 'sovereign people' whom have experienced the most horrific elements of war. They have been through dark and difficult times and emerged as a nation of people full of hope.

Epilogue

In the months leading up to the Kosovo War, NATO used military diplomacy by demonstrating military diplomacy by a show of military force in an attempt to deter Slobodan Milosevic.[88] The Standing Naval Force Mediterranean

---

[88] (Ristic, 2012) Milosevic was indicted in May 1999, during the Kosovo War, by the UN's International Criminal Tribunal for the Former Yugoslavia (ICTY) for crimes against humanity in Kosovo. Charges of violating the laws or customs of war, grave breaches of the Geneva Conventions in Croatia and Bosnia and genocide in Bosnia were added a year and a half later.

The charges on which Milosevic was indicted were: genocide; complicity in genocide; deportation; murder; persecutions on political, racial or religious grounds; inhumane acts/forcible transfer; extermination; imprisonment; torture; wilful killing; unlawful confinement; wilfully causing great suffering; unlawful deportation or transfer; extensive destruction and appropriation of property, not justified by military necessity and carried out unlawfully and wantonly; cruel treatment; plunder of public or private property; attacks on civilians; destruction or willful damage done to historic monuments and institutions dedicated to education or religion; unlawful attacks on civilian objects. The ICTY indictment reads that Milosevic was responsible for the forced deportation of 800,000 ethnic Albanians from

(STANAVFORMED / SNFM) Fleet was operating in both the Mediterranean and Adriatic Seas in the summer and fall of 1998. It was during this time that NATOs Naval Fleet which consisted of the following warships; *ITS Espero* (Italy), *SPS Canarias* (Spain), *HS Macedonia* (Greece), *TCG Karedeniz* (Turkey), *FGS Rheiland Pfalz* (Germany), *HNLMS Van Speigk* (the Netherlands), *HMS Cardiff* (United Kingdom), *USS Kauffman* (United States), and *HMCS St. John's* (Canada) were re-tasked and sent to the Adriatic Sea as an initial show of force and to conduct Adriatic Operations.[89] STANAVFORMED was part of the NATO effort to promote security and stability in the region.

In February 1999, STANAVFORMED was back on station in the Adriatic Sea in response to the escalating situation in the Kosovo region of former Yugoslavia. This presence was critical to the accomplishment of STANAVFORMED's mission as an immediate reaction force for NATO. Just previous to this, during the fall of 1998, I served as a member of the crew onboard *HMCS St. John's* as we conducted Adriatic Operations as a part of NATO's rapid response and show of military force in the region. I consider this aspect of my military service the

---

Kosovo, and the murder of hundreds of Kosovo Albanians and hundreds of non-Serbs in Croatia and Bosnia.

[89] The Adriatic Naval Operations consisted of each nation's vessel being assigned a zone within the Adriatic Sea for which each ship was to maintain, and enforce security by conducting boarding missions of all vessels within their zone. HMCS St. John's Naval Boarding Team (NBT) conducted multiple armed boarding missions during the several weeks that the ship was tasked in the Adriatic Sea.

highlight of my career thus far. Having this connection to Kosovo earlier on in my life and after having had the opportunity to go back to Kosovo for the Balkans Peace Program (BPP) over a decade following the war gave me a chance to observe first-hand the peace building efforts that have been ongoing since the end of the war. I was impressed to say the least at how far Kosovo has come and at the level of stability that now exists in the region.

During the Balkans Peace Program (BPP), the students, including myself had the opportunity to meet with the KSF Brigade Commander at Gjilani City. During which we received an informative briefing on the KSF followed by a tour of the base facilities. Throughout the presentation and tour I was thoroughly impressed by the level of professionalism demonstrated by the commander and his staff. At the end the Brigade Staff was very open to a variety of questions posed by the BPP students. The BPP consisted of multiple such visits with senior government officials and public representatives. These included; the Mayor of Gjilani City, the Minister of Culture, the Minister of Education, the Speaker for the House of Parliament, the Former-President and current Deputy Prime Minister of Kosovo. A common theme that I drew from all these meetings and presentations was that Kosovars are a determined people with a multitude of patience and hope. The leadership has hope in their youthful population; hope that eventually their country with rise in economic prosperity and that the quality of life will improve for all Kosovo citizens. They are also realistic that this economic growth may take decades and they are happy to wait as long as they have their freedom and sovereignty.

The Balkans Peace Program gave me the opportunity to experience the culture and history of Kosovo first-hand. Living there for 3 weeks with a host family whom spoke only Albanian for the most part and being immersed into their culture was a very rewarding and positive experience. To Kosovars, family connections and spending quality family time with your loved ones is one of their highest priorities. The Zeqiri family welcomed me into their lives as if I was a second son, an experience that I cherish. I plan to return to Kosovo with my own family someday soon and allow them to experience Kosovo for themselves.

Kosovars are a 'sovereign people' whom have experienced the most horrific elements of war. They have been through dark and difficult times and have emerged as nation of people full optimism and full of hope. Many of the people that I met were relatively young in age and nearly all were unemployed students.[90] They all remember the war and some spoke with me on their perspective of the events. In reflection, I asked myself how did they survive the war and come through with such

---

[90] Kosovo has a very high unemployment rate, as high as 40-45%.

optimism. Then I recalled how closely the family connections were that I had observed and it was suddenly very clear to me.

> *When life is at its lowest point and you feel like you cannot go on. All we can do is keep breathing and remember the close bond that is 'love'. A bond that we share with those closest to us, this will become the anchor that gives us strength and allows us to survive and carry on.*[91]

References

ACO.NATO.INT. (1999, June 20). Retrieved Sept 15, 2013, from Undertaking of demilitarisation and transformation by the UCK: http://www.aco.nato.int/resources/site7423/General/ Documents/Undertaking%20of%20demilitarlsation%20and%20tra nsformation%20by%20the%20UCK.pdf

ACO.NATO.INT. (1999, June 9). Retrieved Sept 14, 2013, from Miltary Technical Agreement (9 June 1999): http://www.aco.nato.int/resources/site7423/General/Documents/mt a.pdf

---

[91] Quote by Captain Roderick Kelly, written on 28 May 2013, just after crossing the border between Macedonia and Kosovo while travelling north on the M2/E-65 hi-way during the Balkan Peace Program road trip tour of historical and tourist sites of Kosovo, Montenegro, Albania, and Macedonia. The words describe what I believe allowed the Kosovar People to persevere during the darkest times of the Kosovo War while reflecting upon my Post-Conflict Experience during the Balkans Peace Program 2013.

The Kosovo Air Campaign. (2012, March 5). Retrieved Sept 14, 2013, from NATO: http://www.nato.int/cps/en/natolive/topics_49602.htm

NATO.int. (2013, August 20). Retrieved Sept 22, 2013, from Member Countries: http://www.nato.int/cps/en/SID-B1496221-457B7293/natolive/topics_52044.htm

United Nations Interim Administration in Kosovo (UNMIK). (2013, July 30). Retrieved August 23, 2013, from United Nations: http://www.un.org/en/peacekeeping/missions/unmik/

Associated Free Press. (2008, March 20). Bush OKs Supplying Arms to Kosovo.

Aubin, S. (1999). Operation Allied Force : War or 'Coercive Diplomacy' ? *Strategic Reivew: Vol. 27, no. 3,* 4-12.

Biggar, N. (2003). *Burying the Past.* Washington, D.C.: Georgetown University Press.

Campbell, G. (1999). *The Road to Kosovo.* Boulder, Colorado: Westview Press.

Force, T. M. (2010, December 29). *Stand Up, Challenges and Sucess.* Retrieved August 25, 2013, from The Ministry for the Kosovo Security Force - Publications: http://www.mksf-ks.org/repository/docs/Broshura%20ANGLISHT%20%20-%20finale%207.02.2011.PDF

Holzgrefe, J., & Keohane, R. (2003). *Humanitarian Intervention.* Cambridge: Cambridge University Press.

Kabashhaj, S. (2013, January 10). *Kosovo Security Force looks to become an army.* Retrieved September 20, 2013, from SETimes.com: http://www.mksf-ks.org/repository/docs/ Kosovo_Security_Force_looks_to_become_an_army_(anglisht).pdf

King, I., & Mason, W. (2006). *Peace at Any Price.* Ithaca, New York: Cornell University Press.

Ministry for the Kosovo Security Forces. (n.d.). Retrieved May 2, 2013, from Ministry for the Kosovo Security Forces: http://www.mksf-ks.org

Muja, A. (2013). What next for Kosovo Security Sector: KSF an army or not? *Kosovar Centre for Security Studies (KCSS)*, 1-24.

Pettifer, J. (2003). The Kosovo Protection Corps In Transition. *Conflict Studies Research Centre*, 1-10.

Pond, E. (2006). *Endgame in the Balkans.* Washington, D.C.: Brookings Institution Press.

Ristic, M. (2012, September 18). *Balkan Transitional Justice: Dacic Denies His Party's Role in Balkan Conflicts.* Retrieved September 12, 2013, from balkaninsight.com: http://www.balkaninsight.com/en/article/dacic-denies-his-party-s-role-in-war-crimes

Rushiti, V. (2013). The New Kosovo Security Strategy Formulation Process: Inclusiveness and Transparency. *The Forum for Security*, 5.

Vandiver, J. (2013, July 9). *Stars and Stripes.* Retrieved September 28, 2013, from Kosovo security force recognized as fully operational by NATO: http://www.stripes.com/news/europe/kosovo-security-force-recognized-as-fully-operational-by-nato-1.229553

Voorhoeve, J. (2007). *From War to the Rule of Law.* Amsterdam: Amsterdam University Press.

Unique Experiences in Europe's Newest Country

Danielle Gregoire

WHEN I first decided to apply to the Balkans Peace Program I thought it seemed like a great way to finish off my Political Science credits in a much more exciting way than on campus in Edmonton. I applied without much knowledge of the program or of Kosovo as a country. It was a very spontaneous decision. I was attracted to the program due to my interest in conflict resolution, peace building, and post-conflict development as well as the opportunity to experience another country first hand by living with a local family. These all seemed like a great addition to my degree in Political Science, internationalize my degree and gain some firsthand knowledge of the experiences of another culture in a post-war society. I am so glad I chose to do it. I was aware of the political tensions and perpetual conflict throughout the Balkans over the last 100 years; however, I was not highly informed as to Kosovo's role in the conflict or their present political and social situation. I had heard of the country and the war, but that was about it. However, through the program I learned a great deal about the situation unique to Kosovo as Europe's newest country as well as the difficulties it is experiencing despite its newfound independence. In addition to the knowledge I gained from the course materials, I was also lucky enough to have the best homestay experience I could imagine.

When I first looked through the program website and read up a little on Kosovo, my initial thoughts were to be a bit wary. Having seen the movie *Taken* and knowing very little about the country, I was a little sceptical. However, in the end I decided that since I'd heard of the program through the University of Alberta it must be a legitimate opportunity. I did, however, arrive in Pristina half-expecting there to be no one there to pick me up and brought with me the information for a hostel just in case. My preparations were not needed. Instead, my experience in Kosovo and its surrounding countries turned out to be one of the best experiences of my life. I was greeted at the airport by a very friendly young lady holding a large sign bearing mine and the program's name. Festa was 20 years old, very close to my age and extremely warm and pleasant from the moment we met. She welcomed me to her country and I could tell immediately that she was extremely sincere and happy to be hosting me. We got into her cousin's car and began the hour long drive to her home in Gjilan. After stopping at her sister's work where I was again warmly welcomed, we arrived at her home. She lived in what they called a village right outside of Gjilan. By village it was really like a little suburb, only a 5 minute taxi ride from the main streets of Gjilan and the Hotel Kristal. I met her mother and her brothers who were all so genuinely happy to meet me that I knew I could feel at home there and my uncertainty about residing in an Albanian homestay quickly dissipated. My homestay experience was easily the best part of my trip. I learned so much from Festa and her family despite Festa being the only one who could really speak English. Her brothers spoke a few words, but were very shy and relied mostly on their sister to translate. I learned that her father was a construction worker in town and that her mother had been recently laid off due to the bread factory where she worked being shut down. I also discovered that they still owed her six months' worth of back pay that she feared she might never receive. Sharing this kind of personal family information with me made me realize how open and honest Festa was about sharing her life with me.

Upon arriving, her mother immediately asked if I was hungry and prepared me something to eat all while smiling at me like she was just so happy I was there. She instructed Festa to translate to me that while I was in her home I was her daughter and to feel at home and be welcome to anything I needed. Despite not being able to understand any of the conversation going on around me, I could already tell this was going to be such a great experience. For the rest of my stay Festa's mother's face lit up every time I entered a room and she was constantly asking how I was doing and if I needed anything, such as laundry done. Every time I learned a new Albanian word she would get so excited, and we were soon able to exchange greetings in the morning and goodnights before bed. The best moment I shared with her was when the strap on my purse broke and Festa assured me her mother could easily fix it. After a couple days it was returned to me completely stitched up. I asked Festa how to say "thank you for my purse" in Albanian and then ventured downstairs into the kitchen where her mother was preparing dinner. She turned to look at me, and praying that I would pronounce it well enough for her to understand I said "faleminderit per cante" and smiled. She looked at me for a second and then realized that I had spoken Albanian to her and she had actually understood me and got more excited than I have seen someone in a long time. She cheered and gave me the biggest hug, so happy that we had finally been able to communicate more than one word. Small as it was, it was a moment I will never forget.

Another factor I was unsure about before my arrival was the Muslim faith of the country. I had been told previously that 98% of the population was Muslim. However, this was not very apparent at all. I did not expect everyone to be dressed in traditional Muslim attire, but if I had not been told they were Muslim I would not have known. The family drank and took me out to bars, and there were no daily prayers as I had experienced in Turkey where the call for prayer was heard many times throughout the day. Rather I learned that they identified themselves as Muslim, but as Festa's brother-in-law explained to me in broken English, "this is not Afghanistan, women do not wear veils and our country is green and alive". I learned that rather than the characteristics of a strict Muslim society, family values and respect were most important. I remember asking Festa on the first warm day there if it was alright to be wearing shorts that showed most of my legs and she laughed assuring me that it was perfectly fine and that many other girls would be too. The Kosovo fashion was another very neat thing to see, many dressing quite differently than the girls at home in Canada. Again I was made aware of the great importance of family in this society as we walked through the streets of Gjilan. Every 5th person was either a friend of relative of my host sister and we could barely walk ten feet without stopping to say hello to someone and exchange a kiss and a handshake. It was a reality completely different from the busy and indifferent streets of Edmonton where one rarely runs into people they know.

I did notice; however, that gender roles are still quite patriarchal in Kosovo to this day. Festa's mother held the typical domestic female role of cooking and cleaning for the family, while the father went to work. Then when he would come home, dinner would be waiting for him and his needs catered to by the women in the family. I noticed this with the brothers as well.

Whenever they were in the room it was always Festa or her mother who served the tea or offered around food while the brothers sat in the living room watching television. They would also leave the table as soon as the meal was over and leave the women to clean up and do the dishes; except for me because I was a guest they would rarely let me help. By the end I was allowed to help by putting food away back into the fridge, but that was essentially it. Yet, despite these clearly defined gender roles, Festa's family was rather progressive. Festa was a true feminist and I could tell this quite early on from the things that she would say. She treated her brothers as her equals and aside from serving everyone in the room tea she would not wait on them much more. All of the daughters in the family went to school, it was not as though they stayed home learning to keep house while the boys went to school and they all had careers or were working towards them. Festa's oldest sister was a manager at a huge grocery store in Pristina, her sister was a professional dancer, and Festa was studying to be an English teacher and already teaching classes on the side. She was also looking at applying for a United Nations Development Program (UNDP) position in Kosovo geared towards women's empowerment. She asked me to read over the job description and tell her if I thought she was qualified and to look over her application. While I do not believe she had all the qualifications needed, such as experience and a completed university degree, I was nonetheless impressed that she was looking at applying. The position was intended to help the female victims of the war reintegrate into normal life and recover from the loss of family members and the other horrors they had witnessed. It entailed counselling and a means of helping them rebuild their lives. Festa's desire to take on such a position was heart-warming and I told her that she should try, and maybe once she had completed her degree she would have a better chance. With her proficiency in both English and Albanian, as well as her compassionate disposition and feminist attitude, she would do well in that kind of position.

Another cultural difference between Albanians and Canadians that I found very interesting was the way in which birthdays were celebrated. It was Festa's birthday while I was there and she extremely excited to celebrate it with myself and the other exchange students. Although, she was worried that she couldn't afford to have a celebration with everyone, but also did not want to leave anyone out. We were planning on going to a club, so I was not sure what she meant by being able to afford to do this. All she would really have to spend money on would be her own drinks, and she didn't even really drink. Besides, at Canadian birthdays the birthday girl rarely spends any money on her birthday because she will have so many drinks bought for her she won't even know what to do. When I asked her about it and why she was so worried she explained that it is customary for Albanians to foot the bill for everyone when it is there birthday! I found this so shocking. Never in Canada would the birthday girl be expected to pay for everyone's drinks on her birthday, quite the opposite in fact. Even when the two of us went to the grocery store to buy a cake, I was surprised she was buying her own birthday cake and insisted that I would buy it for her because it was her birthday. She was very against this saying no no I must buy it because it is my birthday. In the end I made her let me, but found this custom so different from birthdays back home where the birthday person is meant to be spoiled, not worried that they cannot afford to invite many people to their birthday party because they have to pay for it all. I assured her that none of the Canadians would expect her to pay for anything because that simply was not the way we did it in Canada and so it would not be expected. She was reluctant but I finally convinced her it would be fine and we ended up with about twenty of us at her birthday party. It was such a fun night and she later told me that this was by far the best birthday celebration she had ever had. We also made her a birthday present by printing out a collage of photos of the trip so far and framing it. She was so happy to receive this little gift of memories and it was a good night that I will always remember.

Another thing that I found fascinating about the youth that I met in Kosovo was their obsession with Facebook. Festa was constantly on the site looking through the newsfeed, other people's pictures and liking absolutely everything she saw. Now don't get me wrong, we North Americans waste an infinite amount of time on this social media website as well, but compared to Festa and her cousins and friends, we were barely on it. As soon as Festa added me, I received an average of ten new friend requests every day. From her cousins, friends, and anyone else that I met I would receive a friend request from before the day was over, even people I had never met but who had seen that I was friends with one of their friends. As soon as one of them would post a picture, usually a picture of themselves doing nothing special, they would have about 50 likes within the hour and the number would rise into the hundreds. Here, when I picture is of something awesome or funny, you still will never get nearly that much attention. I quickly learned why as I watched Festa scroll down her newsfeed and like everything she saw. As soon as her birthday was over she immediately wanted my camera so we could post the pictures on Facebook, this was priority number one. Then once we had posted them she watched all day to see how many likes her album got. I was surprised how much Facebook was present in the lives of these young Albanians, and to this day my newsfeed is full of their pictures and I am still constantly surprised at how much attention even the most mundane shots receive. Every night ended with Festa on the computer downstairs or on her phone checking Facebook and how many likes she had received on her latest photo or post. I did also notice; however, that she did often post political statuses about what was going on in Kosovo, as well as later she posted and shared many posts on the protests in Turkey. Her posts were always in support of the Turkish people rising up against the government and she also shared many of her boyfriend's posts as he was heavily involved in politics and interested in other populations rising up against the government.

Skype was another interesting element in Festa's life. I found out that she was part of an English as a second language forum and that she had added many of the people she had met on there to Skype. She would then video chat with these total strangers about their lives, current events in their countries and what they thought about the situation in Kosovo. I found this global community that she had created absolutely fascinating and that she considered these people her friends. She told me that since she is not able to travel, she uses the internet to make international friends and learn about them and their countries. She was talking to a girl from Tiran, who had told her all about the revolution there as well as boy from Turkey who was involved in the protests. After my time in Kosovo, I had a flight booked to Turkey as my next destination and just before my departure the protests broke out. Even though I was not very concerned, Festa was very worried for me and spoke to her Skype friend about the situation and how to keep me safe. I found this very sweet and her friend even offered to meet me when I got there and show me around, when he wasn't taking part in the demonstrations that is. This person was looking up my hostel, sending me links to where the protests were taking place and giving me advice on how to avoid them. I found this very remarkable that a boy that she had never met, but had this friendship over Skype was so willing to help. As someone who has been allowed the opportunity to travel around the world, it made me sad that this was the closest Festa would get to experiencing the world for a while. But it also made me rather impressed that she had found her own way to connect to people of other cultures and different lifestyles across the globe. You learn about globalization and the facility of information travel during classes, but really it is awe-inspiring how the internet allows those who are not physically able to move around to freely to connect and learn from each other.

After settling in to my homestay, classes began on Monday and I met the other program participants. The majority of us were from the University of Alberta; however, there was also a boy from the Check Republic and a girl from London. We began class by learning a bit of background on the war and then looking at the situation in Kosovo today. The class was a mix of international students and local Albanian students who attended the college. This was a fantastic set-up because it allowed us international students to hear the opinions of people around our age who actually live in the country and also allowed the local students to hear our thoughts. It was very interesting to hear some of their views on the topics Professor Bislimi was discussing. One of the most shocking topics we touched on during the course was the subject of unemployment in the country. We learned that Kosovo's population is one of the youngest in Europe and how the huge potential of the youth is essentially being squandered. These youth are getting university degrees but cannot find work afterwards. We learned that the official unemployment rate is around 45%, while the unofficial rate is closer to around 65% because they do not count students in these numbers, despite the fact that many students would like to be working while in school. It also does not include people who are working, but not nearly as much as they would like to, otherwise known as the underemployed. Festa informed me that this is in fact a huge problem and that she herself cannot find even close to the amount of work she would like. She is in the midst of completing her education degree to teach English and while she would like to be working many hours, she can only find 8 hours of work per month teaching kindergarten. Furthermore, this work is in Pristina which requires her to take an hour long bus ride into the capital city every Monday and Wednesday. This works out to two hours of bussing for every hour of teaching, and after deducting bus fare there and back each time, her income is negligible. It was times like these when she would tell me these kinds of things that I felt very guilty for having so many employment opportunities here in Canada, especially living in Alberta. Jobs here are endless and an individual can usually work as many hours as they are willing and able.

We also learned about the huge number of factories that were shut down after the war, which have the potential to be fully functional and provide thousands of Kosovars with jobs to support their families, yet which remain empty and at a standstill. Just like the factory that laid off Festa's mother and still owes her a sum of about 600 euros. The government, I also learned, is doing or nothing or very little to help these workers who have been laid off and who are still waiting to be paid by companies that refuse to even answer their phone calls. I could tell this was stressing out her mother and the family, who I later discovered were still paying off medical bills from when her father had a heart attack two years ago. This news also made me feel uncomfortable and guilty about living in a country where I am so lucky to have universal health care so that a heart attack does not mean a family goes into debt and requires their daughter (the eldest, not Festa) to take out a loan to pay their medical bills. The disproportionate amount of youth in the population, as well as the high unemployment rate was immediately noticeable. Walking down the streets, the cafes were full of young people who were spending their afternoons drinking coffee and chatting rather than working and the young average age was quite visible.

Wondering how these people were able to make ends meet with such high unemployment rates I learned that a large majority of Kosovar family's incomes came from Diasporas. Relatives, who had immigrated primarily to other European countries and North America, were sending money home and allowing the population to survive despite many of them being jobless.

Another shocking element to the Kosovo experience that I discovered was that visa liberalization had still not been achieved. Festa explained to me that it is currently very difficult to acquire a visa to leave the country and travel. They are presently only allowed to travel to Macedonia, Montenegro, Albania and Turkey without a visa due in part to the fear that a large number of them would not return. I found this rather sad as Festa expressed a great desire to travel the world and see other countries, especially the United States and Canada. Especially after hearing the stories of my travels through Europe during my semester abroad she told me how jealous she was and how badly she hopes that one day she will have the opportunity to come and visit me in Canada. I for one, also very much hope that this happens someday and that visas will soon not be so difficult for them to obtain. The European Commission, gave Kosovo a "visa roadmap" on 14 June 2012 which "sets out a comprehensive list of reforms that Kosovo was requested to implement, in order to fulfil requirements related to the freedom of movement, such as reintegration and readmission, document security, border/boundary and migration management, asylum, the fight against organised crime and corruption and fundamental rights related to the freedom of movement". However, the European Union's 2013 Commission report indicates that while "the visa refusal rate for applicants from Kosovo varies across the Schengen area", "the number of Kosovo citizens refused entry to the EU doubled recently". This is made even more difficult because "the authorities in Pristina consider they have fulfilled all criteria for visa liberalisation with the European Union"; however, the above report "maintains a different view... [concluding] that Kosovo's current capacity to fight organised crime and corruption remains limited, with a potentially severe impact on the EU's internal security" (Gaydazhleva). This isolation of Kosovo citizens makes it extremely difficult for them to travel for work and makes life experiences such as the one I had impossible. Especially with the two bodies disagreeing over whether or not the criterion has been fulfilled, progress on the subject of visa liberalization has been slow and tedious.

Another feat that Kosovo still must overcome is that it is still not recognized as an independent country by a number of countries throughout the world. Deputy Prime Minister Edita Tahiri has indicated that "Kosovo has fulfilled all criteria for visa liberalisation" and "[stresses] that the importance of Kosovo's full recognition lies not only in Kosovo's own stability, but also because this would contribute to a sustainable peace and stability in the region, as well as serve the European cohesiveness in foreign policy" (Gaydazhleva). Despite the Republic of Kosovo's declaration of independence from Serbia in 2008, five member countries of the European Union – Cyprus, Spain, Greece, Romania, and Slovakia -- still do not recognize Kosovo as a an independent country (Course notes). This makes inter-country negotiations, trade agreements, partnerships, and development oriented activities extremely difficult. Festa informed me that Kosovo does hope to achieve membership to the EU one day, but has a long way to go before this will ever happen, and wants to do it only on its own terms.

Another very interesting experience during my time in Kosovo was talking to my homestay sister's boyfriend who is extremely involved in politics and very passionate about his country. He works for the VETËVENDOSJE! Movement and spent a lot of time explaining to me his political position and the many changes he would like to see in Kosovo, including self-determination above all. The movement dislikes the extent of foreign involvement from Kosovo and fights to put political power back in the hands of local citizens rather than international actors. He explained that they are not against the international bodies' presence in Kosovo, but that they disapprove of the amount of power these actors' possess. They "think that this presence should be assisting and supporting role especially in social and economic sphere"; however, "the international presence in Kosovo today is itself sovereign" (VETËVENDOSJE! Official Website). They strongly believe that the government of Kosovo, a new and non-corrupt government, should have the final say in decisions that affect the people of Kosovo, not international bodies who ultimately have many interests to consider.

Another aspect of Kosovo's politics that he was passionately against was the privatisation of the countries' industries. He tensely told me that the government was selling off all of Kosovo's industries at rock-bottom prices after which any profits lined the pockets of corrupt politicians to the extreme detriment of the population. He argues that the way in which the government is privatising key Kosovar industries is killing the economy and seriously contributing to the persistently high unemployment rates in the country. They claim that this decentralization is being implemented in favour of Serbian interests rather than Kosovar interests and that Albanians living in Kosovo have to travel further from their homes to obtain the services they need. Festa told me that for serious medical treatment, citizens do not stay in Kosovo but rather must travel to Macedonia for treatment. They argue that the politicians in power today are not truly committed to the development of Kosovo, but rather prioritize appeasing international mandates and more importantly are concerned making concessions that hurt the state and its people while lining their own pockets. The movement maintains that this process of decentralization which has been implemented all over the world by the EU and as conditions for loans by the International Monetary Fund and the World Bank for loans, has failed more often than it has succeeded and is responsible for the downfall of many economies. The privatization process is taking economic and political control and power from Kosovars and their government and giving it to individuals with private interests, none of which is focused on the well-being of the Albanians residing in Kosovo.

When I asked Festa and her boyfriend about the current relationship between Serbs and Albanians in Kosovo, they told me that they are good. Albanians do not hate the Serbs, and the Serbs do not hate the Albanians. However, it was clear from her tone that she was still not too fond of them. It was also clear that there were distinct separations between the Serbian villages in Kosovo and the majority of the Albanian population. They told me that some Serbian villages even use their own Serbian currency rather than the Euro, which is used throughout the rest of Kosovo. Festa commented on this isolation of Kosovar Serbs saying that they choose it themselves and that by continuing to use their own currency and refusing to speak Albanian, even though most of them do know how to speak it, they are hindering their own integration into society. Her boyfriend said that he has nothing against the Serbs living in Kosovo; however, an important part of his political movement's platform is a no more negotiations with Serbia policy matters. He explained (according to his movement) that all negotiations that Kosovo holds with Serbia end up favouring the Serbian minority living in Kosovo or the country of Serbia in regards to territory and border lines. He explained that Serbia still does not recognize Kosovo as a sovereign country and therefore does not recognize their right to self-determination. Until they do this, there cannot be anymore negotiations with Serbia and the members of the movement have protested hard against them. Her boyfriend has even been in jail a few times for his actions during demonstrations against the government and their engagement in negotiations with Serbia. By participating in these negotiations he told me that Kosovo is sacrificing its independence, it sovereignty and its right to self-determination. Instead they should be negotiating issues "such as the common property of Yugoslavia to which Serbia has inherited; reparations payment for war damages caused by Serbia; continued looting of the citizens of Kosovo by the Serbian regime during the 90s; payment for economic damages (physical damage and business of our social enterprises) caused by Serbia during the 90s; troops killed and abducted by Serb forces during the war, who still remain unaccounted for; compensation for colonial exploitation that Serbia has made Kosovo from 1912" (VETËVENDOSJE! Official Website). He was very adamant that the negotiations between Kosovo and Serbia must be about issues that will repair the damages inflicted on Kosovo before, during, and after the war and must stop favoring Serbians, both living in and out of Kosovo. This movement also wishes to unify Albania and Kosovo as one nation in order to create "The Greater Albania".

While I found his views to be slightly one-sided and primarily reflect the Albanian side of the story while mostly ignoring the Serbian side, much of his reasoning against the sovereignty of international actors in Kosovo and the privatization of these industries seemed to have merit. Also there are a few issues such as how they plan to implement this new government and where they are going to get the funding to do all of the things international actors are currently doing in Kosovo, such as operating a military still seem uncertain. There are always two sides to the story and I found that the Serbian side was largely ignored whenever speaking to Festa or her boyfriend about it. However, to be fair, they experienced a war and the destruction of their country and the ethnic cleansing of their people; I imagine that I would also be very bitter toward the country responsible for this. Her father however, did not seem to share this resentment.

My other roommate was from London, but she was half Bulgarian and could speak Bulgarian which I learned was very close to Serbian. Festa's father spoke Serbian fluently and since they were so close, could understand Bulgarian while the

Catherine could understand his Serbian for the most part. They were able to have long conversations during which he told her that he has many Serbian friends who live in the villages and he even took her there to meet them. Festa could not understand Serbian at all, so it was interesting that her father could speak it so fluently and had maintained personal relationships with these Serbian people while she held such resentment for them. I remember her telling me Serbia must send back the bodies that they keep from us. She told us that occasionally they send back a few of them, but that they hold the others when they could send them home. I am not exactly sure what the story is behind this, but it was something that deeply upset Festa that these bodies were kept on Serbian territory rather than being sent home.

Another interesting aspect I found was the love and admiration most Kosovars hold for Americans. Festa has a number of shirts and bags with the American flag on them and speaks very fondly of Americans, while assuring me that they also love Canadians. This love for Americans struck me as odd because throughout all my travels, I have been to 14 countries in Europe, Americans do not necessarily have the greatest reputation. But once I learned the history of the situation between the United States and Kosovo it became much clearer why they felt so warm towards them. From Festa, as well as during class, we learned about the NATO intervention during the mass ethnic cleansing carried out by Serbians against the

Albanians. The United Nations Security Council remained indecisive about what to do and refused to make a solid decision to intervene. Despite this, Bill Clinton attempted to push the authorization for intervention through his own government. Approved by the Senate, but not the House, Bill Clinton still authorized the intervention of American NATO forces in Kosovo thus saving thousands of Kosovar lives. Despite this intervention being extremely controversial because it was never officially authorized by the UN, it was finally ruled as illegal, but justified for humanitarian reasons. I remember in class Professor Bislimi telling us about how a plan for a mass killing of Albanians was discovered later to have been planned for the next day and that NATO's intervention had taken place just in time to prevent this. As a result the people of Kosovo remain forever fond of Americans and especially of their former president Bill Clinton who they consider to have saved them. I remember walking down Bill Clinton Boulevard in Pristina and seeing the large ten foot tall statue of the former president, a symbol of the peoples' appreciation for his help during the war. After learning all of this, I appreciated and understood much better the love of the Kosovo population for Americans.

To conclude, the three weeks I spent in Kosovo amounted to an incredible experience that I will never forget. I was placed with an amazing homestay family who took great care of me and I will consider Festa a friend for life. I am amazed at what she has accomplished despite the hardships that her and her family have experienced both during the war and afterwards. She is an amazing young woman who truly loves her country and believes in its potential to develop and grow into a stronger nation. I sincerely hope that one day it will become possible for her to secure a visa and travel the world, hopefully to Canada where I could host her in return. I learned a great deal from both her and her family, as well as her boyfriend who is currently running for a government position. While I could never completely understand what it is like to live in a post-conflict society, the stories and information from my hosts as well as the information learned throughout Professor Bislimi's course helped me to gain a better understanding of the war in Kosovo and the society that it is now. The potential of the large population of youth in Kosovo is huge and I hope that it will be realized. The young people I met there are educated, ambitious, and truly love their little yet strong country. They have so much to contribute to their society if given the resources and opportunities. For a country with such a grim past, I was amazed at the history, resilience, and unfalteringly optimism that its people carry with them every day.

References

_____. *2013 European Union Commission Report on Kosovo's Progress towards Visa Liberalisation.* February, 2013.

Gaydazhieva, Stanislava. "Kosovo has fulfilled all criteria for visa liberalisation, Deputy PM". NEWEUROPE. October, 2013.

VETËVENDOSJE! Official Website. Frequenty Asked Questions. 2010-2013

Kosovo, What I Saw: An Opinionated Look at the Culture, the History, and the Contemporary Issues of Kosovo's Independence

Evan Klein

Prior

Before I even left for Kosovo I had a mix of emotions and opinions about the country and the trip I would be partaking in. When I first signed up for this journey, I was looking for a travel experience in which I would come back from a progressing area, better educated, more open minded and more capable of making a difference in the world of today. The Balkans Peace Program 2013 fit my wanderlust perfectly. To partake in an academic, international class, I would be going to a country which few know its geographical location, and even fewer actually venture to travel to. I was going to be staying with a host family in a town of 120,000 people (Gjilan), in a republic whose sovereignty is still up for debate. After authenticating the offer to learn abroad, I signed up without hesitation. At this point, I knew slightly what had happened in Kosovo, and what was going on, but not to the extent I would learn on the exchange. This trip was exactly the adventure I had been looking for and I couldn't have been more excited to get on the plane to begin this incredible experience.

It was once I started telling people where I was going that my emotions started to become mixed. When I thought of Kosovo, I thought, a new country, fighting for its sovereignty, but not wasting its time and money fighting each other or holding old grudges. I also thought that the country was stable and my wellbeing wouldn't be an issue. I had quickly checked out some backpacking companies' travel advice, as well as travel Canada's website to confirm what I thought. But other people had a much different perspectives than me. I would tell people where I was going, and they would look at me bewildered, like I was crazy. Some even told me not to go. But after delving deeper as to why they were so amazed, I realized that many people seemed to simply connote Kosovo with fighting, violence, unrest, and 3rd world status because of their violent past. I'm a philosophy/Religion major for a reason: I never know what to believe, and I have a hard time simply accepting a view from one perspective. So now, after having been fairly confident of Kosovo's friendly nature to internationals, as well as the general safety of the country/state, I began to get anxious that maybe people knew something I didn't, and I had gotten myself in over my head…

I could not have been more wrong.!

The Trip

I stepped out of the single terminal of the Pristina airport to lush rolling hills as far as the eye could see, as well as a crowd of tan skinned, seemingly, Albanian people. They generally appeared as slender, dark haired, easily tanned and friendly, but as we all know, the diversity of a country's people cannot be generalized so easily. But this was at a glance, and how I would try to describe a Kosovar to one of my friends if they asked. I didn't know this yet, but the people of Kosovo would forever hold a place in my heart, and I was about to meet the dearest one to me.

At first the pure shock of Kosovo's natural beauty and its people were enough for me to forget that my host brother would be picking me up and driving me to Gjilan. However this stupendous limbo was short lived by my body's betrayal of its own fatigue. I had been traveling for almost 40 hours straight and it was barely morning in Kosovo. I was hungry, tired and anxious about not having any idea where I was or where I was going. All I had was the Bislimi Group's card in my pocket, with a number to call if I really needed. I knew I was fine, but now I was fretting over having to find a phone to contact someone so I could find a snack and a bed an hour away in a country I had never been before. This is when my host brother, Gazmend Azizi, made my day and first introduced himself to me. I knew he wasn't late, and that my plane had come in early, but he still could not have come soon enough. After my stint of 'healthy' anxiety I now felt stable, grounded and rejuvenated: I was ready for the impending unforgettable experience. The first thing that I quickly figured out was how much Kosovars love to smoke. Cigarettes are so unbelievably cheap that it was almost the norm to smoke everywhere, especially since it was allowed in public until the latter end of our trip. The second thing I learnt about Kosovo's people, especially its youth, was how open-minded, accepting, and friendly everyone is. Gozzy (Gazmend) had brought along his own 'personal chauffeur', his friend Valdrin Halimi. Valdrin worked in the government and was an aspiring soccer star before he injured his knee; Gozzy (Gazi, as it is written in Albanian) was an active member of the Central Youth Action Council of Kosovo, as acting vice president, while trying to finish a university degree. They could not have accepted me more graciously into their county.

Within minutes of their introduction I knew that I was going to feel right at home for the whole of the three weeks. The first thing we did was go for coffee, which I assumed was simply because it was only about 9 o'clock and we were all tired. Me a jetlagged traveller, with Gozzy and Valdrin, two university aged gentlemen on a Sunday morning; two things that don't mix. Maybe that time I was right about coffee, but over the next three weeks, I would learn that coffee was more than a pick me up, it was a past time. After we got coffee, I was offered a tour, which would be my first urban look of Kosovo, of Pristina. I gladly accepted. In the state I was in I wasn't overly aware, or able, to take in all that was going on around me. But even so, there were a couple of things I noticed. I couldn't help but notice the communist style buildings as we entered and drove through the city. Apartment block after apartment block of the same grid style buildings; even a library covered with bars, demonstrating the repression of the people. I couldn't help but notice the state of infrastructure, which was sub-par but seemed to be in a state of progress. Buildings looked poorly maintained and cost effectively made. And I couldn't help but notice the love of Americans the Kosovars seemed to have. I was driven down Bill Clinton Boulevard, and shown his 10~ foot statue, depicting him as the hero he was to these people. This was my first glance at Pristina, and although I was tired and the sightseeing was quick, I liked what I saw. It wasn't the buildings, or the infrastructure, or the layout... It was the hope in the people I saw that filled my heart with a love for this country I had barely set my foot in.

I only grew to love Kosovo more and more as the first day went on. After our quick jaunt through Pristina, Valdrin headed the car towards Gjilan, the place I would be spending the majority of my next three weeks. While Gozzy kept trying to suck me into conversation, I found myself unable to take my focus from the landscape that we were traversing through. As far as the eye could see there were rolling hills covered in a blanket of lush greenery, with brick homes splattered sporadically about. It will always be one of my favourite landscapes... Between his mild accent, my fatigue, and my awe of the surrounding backdrop, the conversation was slow. This however, didn't deter Gozzy in the slightest, and he kept me doing my best to try and multitask between thinking, listening, talking and watching; which when you're exhausted, is quite the challenge. After about an hour, we arrived in Gjilan, where my two new friends insisted that we go for coffee at the place to be: Te Papaku. Now I was starting to get the idea of what the life of a Kosovar might be like, but it was only still a glimpse. From what I had seen, it seemed to be a relaxed life that was to be enjoyed in the company of many people, while not having a bountiful amount to do, even if you wanted to. Here, in Gjilan, one thing I learnt quickly, was how in a town of 120000 people, everyone seems to know each other; an unheard of notion in most places I had ever been. In the first day I was probably introduced to 30+ people and all of them, especially my host family, could not have been kinder or more welcoming to me. By the end of my first day I had more friend requests on Facebook than I thought possible, and I felt at home, thousands of miles away from the place I had spent my whole life living. By the first night, all of the worry that prejudiced people had forced me to consider had vanished; and furthermore, I knew that Kosovo was going to be an experience of a lifetime in which I had nothing to worry about.

Almost immediately I started to fall into the swing of things, as a student in Kosovo. We, every weekday, would go to class for 2-3 hours to study peace and post conflict resolution material. Our course was a general introduction to said subject, with Kosovo as the main case study. It was an incredible experience. I was in a class of about forty students of all ages from 4 different countries, with the majority of the class being those who experienced our main topic of study firsthand. I really got to understand the Kosovar side of Kosovo's story.

After thousands of years of simply being the land it was, the area within the boundaries of Kosovo as we know it today, was ruled over by many different government systems attached to just as many different tittles. Whether it was ruled by tribes, Romans, or the Bulgarian or Byzantine Empires, it wasn't until the late twelfth century that Kosovo was 'fully' absorbed into Serbia. But when Serbia fell into fiefdoms and unrest in the 1300's the Ottoman Empire seized the opportunity to expand their territory and took control of both Serbia and Kosovo. After the Ottoman Empire began to decline, and Serbs started displacing Kosovars from their homeland in the russo-turkish war of 1877-1888, there was a large Albanian nationalism movement in Kosovo and the surrounding area. Nearby countries were declaring their independence while Kosovo was still under ottoman control. Then with tensions high in the early 20th century, the Balkan wars occurred. Serbia was looking to expand and, along with other adjacent countries, rid itself of the neighbouring Ottoman Empire. After an Albanian revolt in 1912 the Serbs took their chances and went looking for allies so that they could expand into the area of Kosovo while defeating the Ottoman Empire.

The wars had ended by 1914, with the treaty of London, and subsequently Bucharest with the territory of Kosovo staying under Serbian control. The Albanian population, from Albania to Kosovo, did not see themselves as being liberated in this war however; causing Albania to become its own country, while also fuelling a larger sort of nationalist movement from the Albanians in Kosovo. In hopes of establishing a country free from being ruled, Serbia and surrounding countries came together to form The Kingdom of Serbs, Croats, and Slovenes in 1918. It was renamed to Yugoslavia in 1929. Then after world war two Kosovo was split, as were other areas of Yugoslavia, between the control of countries such as Italy, Germany and Bulgaria. During the years after WWII, there was much conflict between ethnicities within the Yugoslavia area. Kosovo Albanians possibly had it the worst. Starting in the late thirties-early forties they suffered through many war crimes, massacres and what some would even say was genocide. In hopes of preventing further conflict, the new communist government decided not to allow tens of thousands of non-Albanians back into the Kosovo area. And to replace the population, ethnic Albanians took their place. This caused the majority of, the recently declared autonomous region of Serbia, Kosovo, to shift from Serbs to Albanians. The, once again newly named, Socialist Federal Republic of Yugoslavia was in a state of unrest in the 1940's and technically Kosovo was still part of their republic. In 1974 Kosovo was virtually granted self-government, allowing them more freedom and a more ethnically Albanian way of life. It seemed like the tactic of giving the Kosovar Albanians free range over the land as well as a strong Albanian background had deterred the Albanian-Serb ethnic conflict from continuing.

This stalemate of peace all changed in the eighties, when tensions began to rise. Kosovo wanted its sovereignty, and Serbia did not want to lose its territory. What started as protests for liberty became riots, and the Yugoslav government had no problem severely repressing these uprisings. Throughout the eighties Serbs were less and less welcome in Kosovo, as they were being discriminated against as well as attacked because of the way Serbs had treated Kosovars in the past. Then at the end of the eighties, Kosovo's pseudo sovereignty was taken from them, as they lost their privilege to self-govern. Now, as Yugoslavia was breaking up, Serbia, under Slobodan Milosevic, was retaking what they thought was theirs. Specifically, Kosovo.

This ignited the Albanian-Kosovar nationalist movement in explosive fashion. Between not having their autonomous elections recognized as legitimate, as well as the migration of thousands of non-Albanians into their state of recently revoked autonomy, Kosovars saw nowhere left to turn but violence. It was at this point, in the nineties, that the Kosovo Liberation army emerged in hopes of taking back their country's autonomy. Things, however, didn't go according to plan. Between the increase in out of state police, as well as the cooperation between Yugoslavia and Serbia against Kosovo, hate ran high and old grudges were cemented into fruition. A full scale war broke out in 1998, killing tens of thousands of Kosovar Albanians, and displacing hundreds of thousands more. Atrocities were being committed against Kosovo and its people. The war was starting to look less like a two sided battle and more like the genocide of Albanians in Kosovo.

It wasn't until 1999 that NATO finally stepped in to aid Kosovo; and when they did, it was an illegal intervention. When NATO intervened in March of 1999 they did not have UN clearance or sanction to intervene as they did. But even though the organization of the world hadn't given its legitimate approval, it seemed like the world itself did, and the intervention would later be declared as *illegal but just*. Once Serbia surrendered after being bombed for weeks straight, they signed the Kumanovo agreement and control of Kosovo was handed over to the United Nations. Kosovo's future was finally looking up, but it still had a ways to go.

To make sure that the United Nations Interim Administration Mission in Kosovo (UNMVIC) could be carried out in safety, the NATO led Kosovo Force (KFOR) was introduced as the peacemakers of the time. Then after some years of progression, while still theoretically being under Serbian control, Kosovo declared its independence in 2008. The same year, the European Rule of Law Mission in Kosovo was implemented; giving assistance to the KFOR and the UNMVIC initiatives. The problem now for Kosovo was that their independence would not be internationally ratified, as it had to go to a vote in the UN. The reason it has never come to a vote is that even if every country in the UN council agrees upon Kosovo's independence, Russia would veto the decision as they say it undermines the sovereignty of Serbia. It is also thought that if Russia didn't veto Kosovo's liberation, China would, because of their situation with Tibet. This was a brief general part of the history of the country and culture I was immersed in. Like I thought, it was a country striving to gain its independence, but it was caught in a standstill with a generation of transition.

After the couple hours of school each day, we did the only thing there seemed to be to do in Gjilan, eat and drink. The choice of activities was a simple selection, wander the tiny town, go for coffee, or eat the next upcoming meal. So the average day in Gjilan went something like this, with room for manoeuvrability of course: Wake up, coffee, wander to school, coffee, class, coffee, class, wander to lunch, wander to coffer, wander to another coffee place or two or three, dinner, and then wander home. Since the town was so small, it was easy enough to see the majority of the city between coffee shops and on the way to the college. Seeing as Gjilan was so tiny, exploring almost seemed like a dull option after a day or two. And even though I probably could have drawn a half-decent map of Gjilan on my hand, my host brother made sure I knew exactly how to get home no matter where we were. We were tourists and university students though; it seemed odd to me that this life of excessive coffee going seemed to be the norm among people.

Life in Gjilan, and Kosovo, was very different than it is back in Canada, historically and contemporarily. In Gjilan, I could walk everywhere, there wasn't much to do, and one could drive across the country in a couple of hours; contrarily, in Canada (specifically Edmonton), you almost need a car to get around a the city, west Edmonton Mall might have more attractions, shops and restaurants than all of Gjilan, and to get across Canada by plane would be longer than the drive across Kosovo. I was in a place that was nothing like my home, yet I still felt oddly at home when I was there. It didn't take much exploring to notice how stock most of the houses appeared to be. It seemed like everyone had hired the same contractor to build their house, but I knew that wasn't the case. Rather, the reason that most of the houses looked alike was because of the lack of money, most people took the most economical route during the construction process. Buy the cheapest materials, build a simple style house not needing much expertise finishing work, and instead of hiring labour, do as much as you possibly can with family and friends (which puts great emphasis on the simple part). But no matter what time or what day, it shocked me how unbelievably full the cafés were with every type of person. This told me two things: firstly, this confirmed the lack of other options in passing one's time; and secondly, the café crowds exemplified the unemployment rate. It didn't matter what time of day it was, it seemed that most happening cafés were quite busy with middle to old aged men, who would sit around drinking half euro espresso's and smoking cigarettes. Above all though, the café scene tied into the nature of the culture, even humanity, as it expressed people's love, or reliance, of immediate stimulus.

As of now, Kosovo is in a transition stage. They're pushing for their sovereignty and attempting to maintain their state of peace, all while struggling to build up their economy, quality of life and respect to the standard of an EU country. Kosovo has made great strides in becoming what they want to be, with much, needed help from foreign aid… I am in no way trying to undermine what has happened or the progress that has taken place, but there are a significant couple of problems hindering Kosovo's next steps towards autonomy. Firstly, it was easy to look around in Kosovo to see that money was not being used in a way that would help the country progress. People in Kosovo, as is true basically everywhere else in the world, have a tendency to use their money for hedonistic purposes. Hedonism being, the love of pleasure and avoidance of pain; and pleasure comes in many ways, whether it be an espresso, or a cigarette, or the newest phone, or even the newest car. So rather than using their money to better their country as a whole for the future, people look to improve their life now. This mentality can go askew though. At an individual level, this sort of naturally capitalistic mentality usually won't hinder a nation's progress, but will actually stimulate it. So in Canada, spending the money you earn on yourself, stimulates the economy, and theoretically, through the trickle-down effect, strengthens more than just the quality of your own life. Just as in Canada the same is more or less true in any country; any money spent in a country stimulates the economy and the country; but the problem is when this mentality leads to corruption.

Individualistic Hedonism alone won't prevent a country from progressing, but when there is corruption stemming from hedonistic tendencies, major issues arise. Usually when you think of hedonism, you should connote it with utilitarianism, rendering the philosophy bluntly as such: the greatest good for the greatest number is the moral choice; to seek pleasure and avoid pain is ethical. The problem with then calling the Kosovar's, or generally humans, ideology hedonism, is that they only seem to look to improve *their* own pleasure to pain ratio; or the ratio of those who are closest to them. So the better philosophy to attribute to the culture (not saying every Kosovar is like this) would be a niche Cyrenaic Hedonism; where you only look to satisfy your (or your close friends' and family's) pleasure seeking desires from moment to moment. This is where problems arise and corruption begins. It should be noted though, that Kosovars do realize the intrinsic pleasure to social obligation, personal worth, and unselfish behaviour. It just seems that they do not realize the hypocrisy in some of their acts as they are putting their own progress ahead of the progress of their country.

Being immersed in the culture of Gjilan made me realize that even though Kosovars are making an attempt at capitalism they seemed to lack the foresight needed to progress their country. Since most Kosovars are naturally hedonistic, like most other people around the world, everyone is looking to get a leg up on each other, as well as looking to better their life from day to day. One problem with this mentality in Kosovo is that there is a degree of difficulty correlated to increasing your quality of life. This degree of difficulty stems from the opportunities your country gives you. If your country gives you every opportunity, you have much better chances in succeeding, or increasing your quality of life. Here is one major problem of prioritizing personal progress; money is being used to try and improve single lives rather than the country. Most people would agree that Kosovo is not a country that provides an overly generous amount of opportunity for its people, and this lack of opportunity makes improving one's life difficult. So when you walk around Kosovo and see that everyone has the newest iPhone, it hurts you inside, because you understand that they are giving up opportunities of the future, for the pleasures of present. The people believe they can leapfrog their way into the EU or the first world without making any sacrifices. They are people the exact same as you and me, they just don't have the privileges we do, and that exemplifies the faults we have as humans

As mentioned before, individual hedonism usually doesn't tend to prevent a country's growth, unless it is a niche Cyrenaic hedonism that is prevalent in all sects of the country, including the government. This is an aspect of corruption. It's one thing to take the money you have honestly earned and spend it in any way you please, but it is another to shave money out of a budget and into your pocket. It wasn't just the average citizens that would spend their salary on a fancy luxury; it was the government ministers too. Except for the ministers, their budget and their salary are basically synonymous. This means, that if they increase their salary, it comes out of their budget; if they decide to get a new car, it'll probably come from the budget as an expense, etc… This is where the problem of Cyrenaic hedonism gets out of control and becomes an issue of corruption. People, especially government, are taking money, and opportunity, away from their country and their fellow Kosovars so that they can afford a luxury of their own. More than just Kosovars, people seem to fail to realize that until there is progress, for one person to succeed another must suffer.

Another big issue that pertains directly to corruption is the Kosovar's split ideology between capitalism and communism. As a country that just recently fell out of communism, Kosovars realize the errors of its ways, but still tend to hold onto the community aspect of things. I learnt this feature of their ideology quickly, as what's mines is yours, even when it seemed rude to me. My host brother would demand for me to give him my camera; no please, no thank you, just the statement. The first couple of times I was put off by the way he told me to give things to him, but I later realized that if there is a mutual trust between people there is not differentiating what is mine and what is yours. This was a very, very new concept to me. But this community ideology extends to more than just personal belongings; it is a factor in the unemployment rate as well as the corruption of everyday life that Kosovar's seem to think is the norm. Firstly, Kosovar's are accustomed to a society in which everyone had a job and all that had to be done was to meet the quota. Working harder didn't get you more than anyone else, so there was no incentive to work harder. This notion has carried over for much of the older generation. Like most people, Kosovar's want jobs that will give them what everyone else is getting, but requires the minimal amount of work. The problem with this is that Kosovo is now a capitalist country where you are paid for the work you do individually. The lack of individual incentive from person to person is a major factor in the countries unbelievably high unemployment rate which has been upwards of 30%. Secondly, the 'what is mine is yours' mentality is surviving between friends and isn't eradicated in business or government. Looking around Kosovo is was easy to tell that cops didn't give out minor tickets, and traffic laws seemed to be suggestions more than rules. It wasn't rare to hear a Kosovar say that if something or other happened, they would just call someone important they knew to get them out of the situation. Their span of corruption amazed me: from police violations, to people not paying bills, to free services. Corruption means that rather than pay for progress, services, facilities and amenities, you are taking advantage of the system, once again hurting someone else for your own benefit while stagnating the countries development. Kosovar's seem to think that the old communist way of living doesn't hurt their country, and that they can take, what they think is the best, of both communist and capitalist ideologies. The corruption paralleled with the people's conviction to continue to hold communist ideologies in a capitalist country demonstrated why the country is in a transition stage where not much progress is occurring.

Another thing that was easily noticeable was the difference in attitudes between the generation of the future (the large portion of Kosovo's population, that's under twenty four) and their parents who had lived through turmoil and unrest their entire lives. You could feel the hate in the hearts of the older generation. They had lived in a time where they needed their hate to survive. And now that that hate wasn't needed, they didn't know what to do with it. That being said, crime was and is not a major issue because of the ex-communist ideology as well as the Albanian nationalism. No Kosovar would consciously go out and hurt one of their own people. The hate was directed at a different ethnicity, the Serbs, and it seemed this hate couldn't be transformed in any way. These older people's children however, were the optimal example of the generation that broke the cycle of fear, revenge and hate. The new generation of Kosovo, the generation of the future, are open minded, grudgeless, and friendly people. They don't look to the past and see death, destruction and pain, but rather they look to the future and see hope, optimism and a path of progress.

In a previous time, living in Kosovo as a Serb was asking for trouble; now being a Serb in Kosovo is more acceptable. The last century, and more, in Kosovo has harboured an ethnic feud between Serbs and Albanians that quite often saw massacres, human rights violation, people being displaced as refugees and crimes against humanity. It doesn't matter here, which side started the conflict and committed the first gross atrocities; what matters is after the dispute started, neither side had the wherewithal to break the cycle of hate and revenge that kept this feud going. After the conflict had started, and the Albanian population had become the majority in Kosovo in the nineties, the Albanian Kosovars took this advantage as their chance to get even with the Serbs. But rather than get even and end the dispute, they simply continued the cycle of revenge, as they treated the Serbs in terrible ways as well: displacing their people, committing crimes against them, and discriminating against them. When you look at the historical side of the hate, it is easy to see how it has fostered so long in each ethnicity. But being in Kosovo, and spending most of my time with the generation of the future (Kosovars under 25), it was more than plain to see that this generation had broken the destructive cycle of hate and revenge. Rather than looking to get even, which perpetuates the cycle, the youth have come together under one goal, looking towards the future rather than the past. It seems like all that was needed to allow the people to move on with their pain, was a hope that was much greater. The Kosovar youth make up quite a large portion of Kosovo's population; because children weren't usually targeted in war and there was a baby boom after the war ended in 1999. There was more to breaking the cycle than just hope though. The hope needed to be accompanied by a newness, an open-minded acceptance that the part does not represent the whole, and the whole does not fully represent the part. Since some of the youth are so young, they did not experienced the dispute, so hope is all that they needed to move beyond an issue no longer relevant to them. But for the youth between eighteen and twenty five, hope needed to be paralleled with forgiveness, understanding and a willingness to try. Most of these youths understand that there was a two sided cycle of hate, that both sides perpetuated, making it impossible to fully blame one side. Also, they realize that most of the Serbs who performed terrible acts, did so because they were caught in the cycle, or because they had been forced to do so. But most importantly the youth understands that just because Serbia has done terrible things to Kosovo's people, not all Serbians agree with what happened, or even dislike Kosovars. The main idea that broke the cycle of hate and revenge was open-mindedness accompanied with an initial benefit of the doubt. Now rather than seeing a Serbian as a terrible person who should be punished, most Kosovars see Serbians as fellow citizens that deserve every curtsey until proven otherwise. Other than the slightly over zealous international aid, it is the youth of Kosovo that is the reason their country hasn't fallen back into conflict. The youth of Kosovo that is so full of hope, is the hope for Kosovo.

One of the hardest things though, was learning that this generation of the future, was a transition generation; meaning that in their lifetime, they probably wouldn't see much improvement. Every day I was immersed with motivated, loving, hopeful and dedicated members of Kosovo's youth. My host brother was (and still might be) the vice president of Central Youth Action Council of Kosovo, and I even went to their general assembly and was made an honorary member. Being with the youth in Kosovo gave you a glimpse of the hope for the country everyone had, but meeting with the government officials made your heart sink for these hopeful youths.

Over the course of our trip, our program coordinator and professor, Faton Bislimi, did a magnificent job setting up meetings with several government officials. We had the pleasure of meeting with the Mayor of Gjilan, Qemajl Mustafa, with whom we spoke about infrastructure, education and waste management. We meet with the deputy minister of culture, youth and sport, Hajdin Abazi; while also finding time to meet with the deputy minister of education, technology and science, Nehat Mustafa. Faton then went above and beyond, convincing the speaker of parliament to break from his day's meetings to graciously accept our group into his meeting room. What Faton did next though, was more than any of us internationals, or even Kosovar participants, could have imagined. He somehow managed to acquire an invite for our almost twenty person group to the former president, and now first deputy prime minister of Kosovo, Behgjet Pacolli's house. When I say house here, it is one of the grossest understatements of my life. We were invited for an evening to the luxurious estate of Mr. Pacolli, the president and CEO of the Mabatex Group, a high end international construction company. Even before our group went to the estate, I knew this was going to be an experience of a lifetime: not only is his property worth tens of millions of euros, but more importantly to me, Mr. Pacolli has been awarded with more than a dozen honors and awards stemming from his humanitarian efforts. As amazing as it was to be able to see and talk to all of these important government officials in Kosovo; it was this group of people, the older officials that made me realize the standstill Kosovo is now a part.

Talking to these government officials gave me a perspective I had not seen from the hopeful youth I had been around for every second of every day in Kosovo. Talking to the officials made me realize how little the people had to work with. Besides the corruption, and mild misuse of each sector's budget, I was able to see the mentality of a person who was in control of the resources Kosovo offered in improving its own state. What hurt me here is that these people have hope, but not like that of the youth. They see what their money and efforts can do as well as the money and efforts of Kosovo. This was heartbreaking. The government members saw the whole picture and knew that their country wasn't going anywhere fast. The youth had an oblivious hope that was not matched in the government sector; Kosovo doesn't have the necessary resources to propel their country forward. You could feel the almost helplessness of each of the government officials; they seemed to have the mentality that change is coming, but for now we simply must perform our duties.

From talking to the officials, I really realized the stalemate that had occurred in Kosovo and how it all stems from the fact: you cannot force any person to do anything; it must be of their own choosing. The ethnic feud had started because one group couldn't get another group to do what they wanted, so they accomplished their goal by force. While now, Kosovo is in a state where the government would like for people to do things a certain way, or be a certain way, but they cannot force this issue. The stalemate arises now, because it seems that both options lead in a deteriorating direction. The government can't become a system that eradicates Kosovar rights, forcing the people under an oligarchy so that the country may develop; but as of now, the fact that you can't force someone to do something, is preventing their country from progress.

There is so much hope in Kosovo, but the country is not unified in its direction of progress. There are too many people that are simply looking out for themselves and their families while not considering the effects that correspond to the country. The Rule of law is affected because of the corruption; laws are not upheld because many cops let family, friends, and even friends of friends off easy. Bills go unpaid because company workers won't let their friend's, family's or friend of friend's water/gas/cable/electricity be turned off. This means that while the rule of law of the country is being undermined, so is their capitalist progression. Forcing people to do something creates a problem, but allowing people to maintain their destructive ways does not help the situation either. You need a rule of law to progress a country but when corruption undermines the rule of law, even the established rules aren't being upheld, never mind the un-established ideals. Kosovo is in a tough situation, and that is why they call the generation of the future, the transition generation.

Going to Kosovo was one of the best choices I have ever made in my entire life. I went there with hopes of becoming a better person; socially, personally, and intellectually. Kosovo did so much more than what I had hoped. I met so many great people that I know I will stay in contact with for the rest of my life. Whether they were from Canada, Europe, or Kosovo specifically, I have never been in better company for three weeks. This trip also taught me about what I really care for and want to see in the world. Staying in Canada doesn't open your eyes to the things that are going on the world. Most mainstream media is biased, using rhetoric and covering selective stories to meet their own agendas; giving you a skewed, or wrong, perspective of what is going on in the world of today. But travelling to other countries, especially countries that need help, really makes you realize the luxury we live in while other people are suffering. Going to Kosovo made me realize that sitting at home saying the most basic ethical principle is: everyone deserves equal opportunity from birth; is no better than anyone who doesn't realize that. What is truly ethical is going out there and attempting to make the world into a place where opportunity is equal. Besides opening my eyes to my back-seat ways of hoping for a better world I had been caught up in, the Balkans Peace Program 2013 made me more able to be the person I want to be, rendering my abilities more apt to help others. But, the trip wasn't only just spiritual and intellectual; there was much fun to be had.

When we weren't in school, we had the opportunity to travel all around the Balkans. One weekend we spent a day having a barbeque on top of a hill with a magnificent sight, playing soccer and basketball. Another day, we spent the entire day touring around Kosovo, where we saw the Castle town of Prizren, some underground caves and an unbelievable waterfall. That wasn't the extent of our travelling though. We went to Skopje Macedonia, Tirana, Pogradec, and Durres, Albania, and Ulqin, Montenegro. Between days at the beach, scenic drives, tours and lots of laughs, the mini trip was an absolute blast; but I always seemed to miss the homeliness of Kosovo and Gjilan. I fell in love with Kosovo even though I didn't try....

I have never been more accepted or loved in a new community in my entire life, than I was in Gjilan. I can't thank Faton and the Bislimi Group Foundation enough for the opportunity they gave me. I miss Kosovo and my Kosovars every day that I'm back home. This trip made me realize how much more can go on in a country than I even dared to think about initially. It forever opened my eyes to the good nature of people, while making me realize that even with the best intentions things can still get horribly wrong. My love for Kosovo is unwavering, and I hope the country and its people all of the best.

EPILOGUE

Viewing the world through the lens of isolation stymies one's potential for socio-cultural growth. As the 21st century unfolds, possessing an awareness of the world is more important than ever as the multifaceted globalization of today's world sets the stage for tomorrow. Cross-cultural and educational exchanges provide young people an immense opportunity for substantive and transformative experiences through which sow seeds for global citizenship through the establishment and development of eventual international partnerships. It is through individual and collective education that the shackles of disparity, conflict, and animosity can be reduced and real growth can occur. Moreover, as Europe's newest democracy, Kosovo and the Kosovars themselves are at a crossroad – a downward spiral deeper into the abyss of cronyism, corruption, and instability where the nouveau riche prosper at the expense of the public at-large; or, as a leader in Balkans' 21st century transformation into a major regional contributor to peace, industry, agriculture, and business development. Educational experiences for young people, such as the Bislimi Group Foundation's *Balkans Peace Program* provides, in part, one such example of substantive and transformative exchange experiences for Westerners and Kosovars alike for building a new foundation for peace and stability in the Balkans sans the socio-political and economic umbilical cord of N.A.T.O. and the European Union. Education and exchange experiences are a critical element in preparing the youth to lead tomorrow's Kosovo. For the sustenance of Kosovo is not a political, economic, or social script presented by the European Union or the United States -- but rather its youth as they move forward and continue to build and shore-up a democratic Kosovo. While Kosovo's independence and democratic systems are an appreciated legacy of the support from the International Community and United States in particular, Kosovars must become equipped to develop and sustain their newborn democracy on their own devices. In an effort to accomplish this, educational exchange programs fostering peace, reconciliation, conflict resolution, and democratic partnerships provide fertile ground for re-establishing a sense of regional connectedness, identity, and stability by exposing Westerners to the Balkans (and vice versa).

Dr. Eric Franco
Waldorf College
16 June 2014

Quotes from the Balkans Peace Program 2013

"It is always a pleasure to meet with students. You are tomorrow's leaders. I hope that your experience in Kosova while on this important summer educational program has been a great one. I thank you for visiting our country and I also thank Professor Bislimi for doing such a great job on a volunteer basis with this summer program."
Dr. Jakup Krasniqi
Speaker of the Parliament of Kosovo

"I welcome you to Kosova and to my own home. When Professor Bislimi told me he had a group of foreign students staying in Gjilan for the Balkans Peace Program, I immediately asked him if I could have the honour of hosting you for dinner at my own place one evening. So, I am glad you could make it. I am sure your experience in our country will be an unforgettable one. You are in great hands..."
Mr. Behgjet Pacolli
Former President of Kosova
First Deputy Prime Minister of Kosovo

"There is no better way to understand a people than by becoming part of their daily lives. The Balkans Peace Program offers you the opportunity to become part of our daily, family lives in Kosova. I am very glad you chose to participate in this program, and I have looked forward to this meeting with you. So, I welcome you to Kosova and the Government of Kosova."
Mr. Nehat Mustafa
Deputy Minister of Education, Science, and Technology
Government of Kosovo

"The Balkans Peace Program gave me the opportunity to experience the culture and history of Kosovo first-hand. Living there for 3 weeks with a host family who spoke only Albanian for the most part, and being immersed into their culture was a very rewarding and positive experience."
Cpt Roderick Kelly
Royal Military College of Canada, BPP 2013 Participant

"I have never been more accepted or loved in a new community in my entire life, than I was in Gjilan. I can't thank Faton and the Bislimi foundation enough for the opportunity they gave me. I miss Kosovo and my Kosovars every day that I'm back home. This trip made me realize how much more can go on in a country than I even dared to think about initially. It forever opened my eyes to the good nature of people, while making me realize that even with the best intentions things can still get horribly wrong. My love for Kosovo is unwavering, and I hope the country and its people all of the best."
Evan Klein
University of Alberta, BPP 2013 Participant

"The Balkans Peace Program gave students like myself a chance to be immersed directly into the Kosovar life fourteen years after the war had taken place. We were able to see how students around our own ages lived in a post war society, and hear from the locals how the war affected them, at the time and currently, and what the government was doing to help. At the same time we did get to have in depth meetings with members of the Kosovo government to hear how they have arranged budgets and created programs in order to help rebuild their country's economy."
Anneka Sutton
Sir Wilfrid Laurier University, BPP 2013 Participant

"The three weeks I spent in Kosovo amounted to an incredible experience that I will never forget. I was placed with an amazing homestay family who took great care of me and I will consider Festa a friend for life. While I could never completely understand what it is like to live in a post-conflict society, the stories and information from my hosts as well as the information learned throughout Professor Bislimi's course helped me to gain a better understanding of the war in Kosovo and the society that it is now. For a country with such a

grim past, I was amazed at the history, resilience, and unfalteringly optimism that its people carry with them every day."
Danielle Gregoire
University of Alberta, BPP 2013 Participant

"My time in Kosovo on the Balkans Peace Program was an eye-opener for the struggles that people have to make on daily basis to move on with their daily lives. Coming from Europe and going to Europe's newest country, this was an important lesson for me. I enjoyed every minute there and I plan to return as soon as I get a chance again."
Milan Zavada
Charles University (Prague, Czech Republic), BPP 2013 Participant

www.ingramcontent.com/pod-product-compliance
Lightning Source LLC
Chambersburg PA
CBHW031512270326
41930CB00006B/375